HEARING THE MESSAGE OF ECCLESIASTES

QUESTIONING FAITH IN A BAFFLING WORLD

CHRISTOPHER J. H. WRIGHT

ZONDERVAN

Hearing the Message of Ecclesiastes
Copyright © 2023 by Christopher J. H. Wright

Published in Grand Rapids, Michigan, by Zondervan. Zondervan is a registered trademark of HarperCollins Christian Publishing, Inc.

Requests for information should be addressed to customercare@harpercollins.com.

Zondervan titles may be purchased in bulk for educational, business, fundraising, or sales promotional use. For information, please email SpecialMarkets@Zondervan.com.

ISBN 978-0-310-14746-6 (audio)

Library of Congress Cataloging-in-Publication Data

Names: Wright, Christopher J. H., 1947- author.
Title: Hearing the message of Ecclesiastes : questioning faith in a baffling world / Christopher J. H. Wright.
Description: Grand Rapids : Zondervan, 2023.
Identifiers: LCCN 2022058134 (print) | LCCN 2022058135 (ebook) | ISBN 9780310145912 (paperback) | ISBN 9780310147459 (ebook)
Subjects: LCSH: Bible. Ecclesiastes--Criticism, interpretation, etc. | Faith (Christianity) | Life—Biblical teaching. | BISAC: RELIGION / Biblical Studies / Old Testament / Poetry & Wisdom Literature | RELIGION / Biblical Studies / Exegesis & Hermeneutics
Classification: LCC BS1475.6.F3 W75 2023   (print) | LCC BS1475.6.F3   (ebook) | DDC 223/.806—dc23/eng/20230421
LC record available at https://lccn.loc.gov/2022058134
LC ebook record available at https://lccn.loc.gov/2022058135

Cover design: Studio Gearbox
Cover photo: © Dutchinny / Getty Images
Interior design: Kait Lamphere

Printed in the United States of America

HB 05.20.2024

To the Cornerstone Campers

CONTENTS

PREFACE

The very first book I ever published included a small commentary (of sorts) on Ecclesiastes, long since out of print. It was a Scripture Union Bible Study Commentary on *Proverbs–Isaiah 39* (London: Scripture Union, 1983). Shortly after it was published a friend told me that he was still a Christian only because of Ecclesiastes (the biblical book, you understand, not my commentary). "I had reached the point of almost suicidal despair at the pointlessness of life in general," he told me. "Then I read Ecclesiastes, and I found him saying exactly what I was thinking. So I thought, 'If God allowed him to say those things and to have them actually in the Bible, maybe it's worth hanging on a bit longer.'" He is probably not the only one who has found Ecclesiastes to be the most ruthlessly honest book they've come across and so been able to cling to their faith as the book itself does.

Reading my small commentary nearly forty years later, I am relieved to find that I still agree with myself. Back then, this is what I wrote:

> Ecclesiastes pushes to its uncomfortable limit a tension . . . between a vision of the world as it ought to be, with righteousness prospering and wickedness confounded, and observation of the world as it is, with its injustice and absurdities. The first is the voice of faith in the character and promises of God; the second is the voice of harsh experience. And it is the strength with which the faith in God's revelation is held that produces the agony over the state of the world. The world poses no great *moral* problem for the atheist (why should it

be other than it is?), or for the polytheist (what else can you expect with a chaos of rival gods?). But for one who accepts the revelation of *one, good, sovereign* God, it *is* an enigma. (p. 50)

Now, I am well aware that there are many and varied ways of reading Ecclesiastes and a plethora of commentaries that offer them. There are different views of how many voices speak within it; whether the voices agree or disagree with each other; what the author is "really trying to say"; whether there is any intentional structuring; whether there is a definite historical background to the book, and if so, what it is; and so on. I have not attempted to discuss or resolve any of these questions. I simply want to accompany the author in his rather meandering pilgrimage (if that's what it is).

I happily acknowledge that my approach is heavily dependent on that of Craig Bartholomew,[1] since I find myself broadly convinced by his reading of the book as a journey or quest, in which its main character seeks to understand the meaning of life as far as he possibly can with the tools of his own empirical observation and reason. It is a quest that takes him to some crunching dead ends, but also to some moments of remarkable insight. And it is a quest that eventually reaches some positive reflections and words of advice, without satisfactorily resolving some of his hardest questions—for which we need the rest of the biblical story and its fuller revelation.

Regarding this complex book in the wisdom literature of the Old Testament, it would be foolish to claim that this is the "right" or "best" or "only" way to read Ecclesiastes, and I make no such claim. All I can say is that I have found it helpful to imagine myself accompanying the writer on his quest. It is a quest that has some disorientating twists and turns and the occasional complete *impasse*,

---

1. Craig C. Bartholomew, *Ecclesiastes,* Baker Commentary on the Old Testament Wisdom and Psalms (Grand Rapids: Baker Academic, 2009).

but that eventually arrives at journey's end. The book reaches a conclusion that, however incomplete in itself, I find broadly positive when placed in the light of the whole scriptural narrative.

I am grateful to All Souls Church, Langham Place, London, for inviting me to begin each day of the church summer camp ("Cornerstone") in August 2017 with expositions of Ecclesiastes (which the cheerful campers daily denounced as "Meaningless! Meaningless!" for which the dedication grants absolution). This book is substantially an expansion of what I delivered at that event.

Somehow, the message of Ecclesiastes seems remarkably contemporary, challenging, and strangely reassuring when we submit our faith to testing questions, as Qoheleth did, in a world that is still as baffling to us as it was to him.

Chris Wright
Summer 2021

INTRODUCTION

"And I think to myself, 'What a wonderful world!'" Louis Armstrong's classic song finds an echo in our hearts whenever we too encounter the things he lists in the lyrics: trees of green, red roses, skies of blue, clouds of white, the colors of the rainbow, friends shaking hands, babies growing and learning. . . . Yes, all of them wonderful in their own way, from the vastness of creation to the miniature joys of babyhood. It's not just sentimental. It is the appropriate response of sheer gratitude for so much that fills us with pleasure and amazement, mediated to us by the world we live in. And if we are Christians, we can sing it with the psalmists to the Creator God himself, "What a wonderful world!"

But there are times, perhaps as many, when other songs speak for our mood more painfully: like Bob Dylan, *"Everything is broken . . . ,"* or Leonard Cohen, *"There is a crack, a crack, in everything; that's how the light gets in."* And the psalmist can sing those songs, too, with us and for us.

> Help, LORD, for no one is faithful anymore;
> > those who are loyal have vanished from the
> > > human race.
> Everyone lies to their neighbor;
> > they flatter with their lips
> > but harbor deception in their hearts. (Ps 12:1–2)

> How long must I wrestle with my thoughts
> > and day after day have sorrow in my heart? (Ps 13:2)

How often have I watched the news of the latest bloody atrocity, or horrendous accident, or natural disaster, or grieved over the suffering of the poor of the earth alongside the arrogance of the super-wealthy, or been enraged by the hypocrisy and corruption of our political leaders, and think to myself, "What a terrible world!" What a crazy, unfair, miserable, violent, cruel, baffling world!

But I'm a Christian believer, and part of my belief is that this is God's world. Shouldn't that make it easier? Actually, it only makes it harder, since if God is the God of sovereign power and love, as the Bible says, then how did we get a world like this?

Some years ago, I wrote a book entitled *The God I Don't Understand: Reflecting on Tough Questions of Faith.*[1] It addressed negative things that are hard to understand in relation to God, like the problem of suffering and evil and the violence of the Old Testament, and also positive things that we put our trust and hope in without being able to claim full understanding, like the cross of Christ and the future destiny of our universe. That book wrestled with some questions, not attempting to answer them all with convincing arguments and clear-cut solutions. Far from it.

This book is also a wrestling. But this time I've got company. I have enlisted the writer of the book of Ecclesiastes and its main character (whose name, Qoheleth, I'll explain in a moment) for a journey of questioning faith. They came from the community of the wise in Old Testament Israel, a tradition that also gave us the books of Proverbs and Job. These were men and women whose voices were quite different from those of the prophets. Wisdom and prophecy were recognized in Israel as two of the three valid but distinct ways of receiving truth from God. The third was the teaching of the priests. This trio of "authorized" voices was identified by the enemies of Jeremiah, who reckoned that killing

---

1. Christopher J.H. Wright, *The God I Don't Understand: Reflecting on Tough Questions of Faith* (Grand Rapids: Zondervan, 2008).

him (just one less prophet) would not make much of a dent in the availability of divine instruction.

> They said, "Come, let's make plans against Jeremiah; for the teaching of the law by *the priest* will not cease, nor will counsel from *the wise*, nor the word from *the prophets*."
> (Jer 18:18; my italics)

The wise spoke with insight derived from experience and rational reflection. Prophets spoke with more direct insights received from God. But both could struggle and wrestle exhaustingly with the agonizing challenges of the world they saw around them. Some of the questions we confront in Ecclesiastes find echoes in the struggles of Jeremiah or Habakkuk as they agonized over the meaning of God's words and actions in a world they could not fully understand. Just as we do. Wisdom and prophecy both give us permission to ask hard questions, and so do many of the Psalms (e.g., "How long, Lord?").

QUESTIONING FAITH

"Questioning faith." The first word is deliberately ambiguous, whether faith is its object (addressing questions to our faith) or its subject (a faith that is strong enough to ask hard questions). There is no doubt at all in my mind that Qoheleth was a person of faith, a believer in the God of Israel. But his faith could hurl tough questions: questioning God and questioning the received wisdom of his own people. And at the same time, he was bold enough to question faith itself—to pose the awkward, challenging question: "If you believe God is like that, how can the world be like this?" In other words, Qoheleth allows faith to ask questions and hurls questions at faith itself.

And he does this precisely because there is so much about the world that is not always "wonderful" but very often baffling and disturbing. It is a world that Qoheleth says he can't understand because it is full of inexplicable enigmas, unfair outcomes, and the black hole of death that seems to render even the best things of life pointless and meaningless. And yet, and yet . . . it is still a good and wonderful world in which we work, eat, drink, enjoy life, make love . . . and all with God's smile. How can both be true? Qoheleth believes that both are indeed true but struggles to understand how they can be reconciled, if at all.

In a world he can't fully understand, Qoheleth circles around an abyss of nihilism and pessimism (the world baffles him), yet he remains a believer. Faith wins. Not a "happy clappy" superficial faith that denies or ignores the baffling and frightening realities of our world, but faith that can live with unanswered questions and go on trusting the living God, faith that invites his readers to do the same.

I have found that Ecclesiastes, along with equally tough books like Habakkuk and some of the lament Psalms, speaks to my heart in recent years. There is so much about our world that is both baffling and terrifying. The future seems more uncertain than ever—or rather, some things seem all too ineluctably certain, like the climate chaos of global warming and its impact on the whole human race as well as the natural order. So I resonate with the way Qoheleth just "tells it like it is," or when a prophet like Habakkuk boldly pounds God's chest with his questions and complaints. And then I find comfort in the way both of them journey forward to a place of trust and affirmation. It's a bumpy journey. But it's well worth traveling alongside.

THE BOOK'S CENTRAL CHARACTER

Allow me, then, to introduce you to my friend Qoheleth (pronounced Ko-HEL-eth). Actually, that's not his name; it's not really a personal name at all; it's more like a title or a job description. The word in Hebrew may mean somebody who gathers the assembly or congregation (*qahal*). That's how we got the rather clumsy and off-putting English title of his book, "Ecclesiastes" (from the Greek translation, *ekklesia*, the assembly, or later, the church). But what would he gather people for? Probably in order to address them with his teaching or challenge them with his reflections and questions. Or it may mean "the Gatherer," that is, somebody who collects the wisdom and proverbs of others and puts it all together in lectures and books (which would fit the way he is described in 12:9–12). The NIV calls him the Teacher. We might think of him as the Philosopher, or the Professor, or the Pundit. But I prefer just to use the name or title that his book itself gives him. So from here on, we'll call him Qoheleth.

Qoheleth is clearly a very strong believer in God. He stands within the wisdom tradition in Israel and shares the profound monotheistic convictions of Israel's faith. And, rooted in Israel's belief in the one true living God as Creator, he has an amazingly positive view of the goodness of life and work, food and wine, sex and marriage, investment and wealth, and so on. God is good. Life is good. That is the undergirding certainty that he affirms again and again—seven times in all, to be precise.

But yet, Qoheleth sees (as we all do) that all of those things can go horribly wrong. Life can also be a complete mess, or absurdly unfair, or just plain baffling. God is presumed to be in sovereign control, but does it look like it all the time? Qoheleth tries desperately hard to understand the world, using all the rational means at his disposal, but keeps on coming back to the same conclusion. He can't understand. It's all just meaningless—or is it? He wrestles with the apparent futility of life and the awful finality of death. So he hates life, but still loves life, and tells us why on both sides.

Here then is somebody who knows what he believes in his head but struggles to cope with what he sees with his eyes and feels in his emotions.

Somebody just like most of us, to be honest.

THE BOOK'S STRUCTURE AND VOICES

The book comes to us as a kind of double act. There are two voices.

1. **The Frame-Narrator.** The book opens and closes by its author telling us that he is reporting the words of Qoheleth. He introduces Qoheleth in 1:1–11. Then he reports what Qoheleth said, from 1:12 through the whole central part of the book (with a brief reminder that this is what he is doing at 7:27). The narrator then finishes the book off in 12:8–14. So those opening (1:1–11) and closing (12:8–14) sections make up the "frame" for the book. Consequently, the overall author, or editor, of the book as a whole is sometimes called the "Frame-Narrator."
2. **Qoheleth, "I, the Teacher . . ." (1:12).** This is the autobiographical substance of the book. Qoheleth speaks in the first person throughout (except for 7:27) until 12:8.

So there is a "frame" and a "testimony." The actual author/editor of the book is telling us what he heard Qoheleth say or teach, reporting and recording it for us but not necessarily *approving* of it all. Indeed, some think that 12:8–14 is a gentle critique of Qoheleth: "He tried but didn't succeed." If it is, it is very gentle indeed. On the whole, I think the concluding verses of the book are not *denying or correcting* Qoheleth but reminding us of some fundamental convictions that we must hold on to as we reflect on his words. Qoheleth goads us into hard thinking about hard questions, but we must do that thinking and questioning within the secure framework of biblical faith and godly living.

That's why we need to be careful not to think that we are expected simply to agree with everything that Qoheleth says just because, well, "it's in the Bible." This is like when we read the reported speeches of Job's friends, and even of Job himself. We are not necessarily expected to agree with all they say in the context of the message of that book as a whole and the wider truths of the whole of Scripture. We need to take seriously what Qoheleth says at every point of his journey or quest. But sometimes we must suspend judgment on whether he's right or not until we get to the end of the book and can evaluate his quest and his provisional conclusions along the way in the light of chapters 11–12.

Who then was Qoheleth? He is introduced as a "son of David, king in Jerusalem" (1:1) and says he "was king over Israel in Jerusalem" (1:12). That sounds like Solomon, and the book used to be attributed to him. But is it? Several aspects of the book make it unlikely, if not impossible, that the historical Solomon was the author. Some things are just rather odd. For example, he says that he grew wiser than anyone who had ruled in Jerusalem before him (1:16). Well, that was only one person, David! And why choose a strange non-personal name—"The Teacher/Preacher/ Pundit"—rather than Solomon's actual name, like the book of Proverbs? And the "Solomon" flavor disappears after chapter 2.

More significantly, the Hebrew of Ecclesiastes is "late Hebrew," with many Aramaisms (words or constructions that reflect the shift from Hebrew to Aramaic among Jews in the later centuries). Certainly, it is a much later form of the language than the Hebrew of centuries earlier (Solomon was tenth century BC). This is not a clinching argument, since the language of ancient books can be updated for later times (like our modern Bible translations). But it goes along with another consideration: that some of the issues and perspectives of the book seem to reflect the influence of Greek philosophy, and that would point toward a date when the Jews lived under Hellenistic rule in the postexilic era.

Many scholars and commentators are of the view that Qoheleth is speaking (at least at the start of the book) *in the guise of Solomon*—in an accepted and understood way. That is, he is imaginatively por-traying what Solomon could have done and thought. Solomon was legendary as the great patron of the wisdom, arts, and science of his era; a skillful political administrator; an energetic initiator of many infrastructure projects; one who amassed great wealth through international trade and multiplied marriages of diplomatic advantage; and so on. Solomon had all the time, resources, money, and opportunity to find the meaning of life. If anybody should have found the key to understanding the world and leading a successful, fulfilling, and *meaningful* life, it should have been Solomon. "But," says Qoheleth (speaking as Solomon), "I didn't."

So if Qoheleth was not Solomon, then who was he? The fact is, we don't know. He has chosen to be anonymous. It is perfectly possible that he was a historical person whose struggles, reflections, questions, and insights have been recorded and reported by the author of the book, the "Frame-Narrator," with his introduction and final comments.

THE BOOK'S MESSAGE—A QUEST

There have been many different ways of reading and interpreting Ecclesiastes over the centuries. It is not easy to discern a clear structure, or to be dogmatic about whatever structure we may think we can outline, still less to state a single, simple clear and central message. However, as I said in the preface, I have found it helpful and stimulating to follow Craig Bartholomew's reading of the book as a kind of journey, a quest. This is suggested by the rather autobiographical way Qoheleth launches into his argument in 1:12–2:26. But it is also set up by the question that the Frame-Narrator puts right up front in 1:3:

> *What do people gain from all their labors*
> *at which they toil under the sun? (1:3)*

We shall look at the full meaning and implications of that in chapter 1 below, but at this point it's worth taking this verse to be the key question that the book addresses. And in one sense, it seems to be a rhetorical question, expecting a depressing answer, "Well, nothing at all really." But in another sense, it feels like an invitation: "Let's try and find out. . . ." The answer may turn out to be the same in the end (who knows at this stage?), but the quest is on. Let's watch

Qoheleth, the Frame-Narrator says, as he explores every avenue of life, private and public, to answer that question. Let's journey with him as he strives to find out if there is any way to grasp the meaning and value of life by human wisdom and exploration alone.

This way of reading the book—as a journey or quest—also means that we should not judge every verse on its own along the way, as if it is making a definitive statement that we must accept as true. Qoheleth is poking and prodding conventional wisdom and theories, trying things out, observing multiple situations and events, making a great mental effort to get his head around the baffling enigmas of life. And that leads to a feature of the book that we really must keep in mind.

THE BOOK'S METHOD: IRONY AND PARADOX, GAPS AND CONTRADICTIONS

This can be the most puzzling aspect of the book. Qoheleth seems to say things that are contradictory. At times he contradicts himself; at other times he seems to contradict core parts of Israel's faith. And we need to understand this is almost certainly conscious and *deliberate*! He is forcing his listeners/readers to *think*. He is slapping us in the face, to wake up and get real, not to be content with trite answers or smart proverbs. He wants us to see the absurdities of life, when things happen that are completely illogical and make no sense. Sometimes he uses irony: "common wisdom says *this*, but *the opposite* seems to be true at least some of the time." Sometimes he uses paradox: "you'd think this should be the case, but things can turn out surprisingly contrary to all expectations." Sometimes, he just puts opposites side by side without comment, leaving us to try to find a way to bridge the gap in between them—especially if the opposites contradict each other and yet each seems to be true in its own way. We need to recognize this *genre* of literature and its methods. Don't read it as you would, say, John's Gospel.

And the most extreme apparent contradiction that threads

through the book is that in some verses he can be saying that life is pointless, then you die, so you might as well not have been born at all; and in the next breath he is saying that life is good (nothing better), a wonderful gift of God for us to enjoy to the full. And he challenges us to wrestle with that mystery. Is it one or the other? Or both? Is there an answer? Is there a key, a clue, a solution to the baffling enigmas of this world he cannot understand? Well, if there is, it is not one he can find by rationality and wisdom and observation alone.

And nor can we.

For as we know from the rest of the biblical canon (and as Qoheleth could have known from the Scriptures of Israel available to him), we need God's revelation of himself and his creation, alongside God's diagnosis of the human condition, to even begin to understand the world we live in. Not that such revelation instantly "solves" all the problems that Qoheleth wrestles with or provides neat answers to every question he asks. But it is the framework within which that wrestling and questioning must take place.

At its simplest, the book of Ecclesiastes is trying (whether consciously or not in the mind of the author and Qoheleth) to work out how Genesis 1–2 can be true and good in a world full of the results of Genesis 3. For the book gives strong affirmation of both the truth of the world as created by the one, living, sovereign God in Genesis 1–2, and the facts of the world as ravaged by the outcomes of Genesis 3—outcomes such as the flimsy transience of a human life, even a long and apparently fulfilling one; the unknowable abyss of death and forgottenness; the anger of injustice and tears of suffering; the accidents and unpredictability that confound all rational expectations; and so on. All these things seem to prevent any lasting or absolute meaning to life, even when you know that life is in itself a good gift of God.

There is a good world we love and enjoy.

And there is a baffling world we don't understand.

But it's actually one world, and we have no choice but to live with the tension.

THE MEANING OF LIFE—
IS THERE ANY?

Ecclesiastes 1:1–2:26

So let's plunge straight in. "Plunge" is the right word. Like into an ice-cold lake. The author's brutally direct opening is deliberately shocking. In just two verses he throws out the assertion (v. 2) and asks the question (v. 3) that will dominate our wrestling brains all the way through the journey of this book.

THE CHALLENGE OF LIFE (1:1–3)

> *"Meaningless! Meaningless!"*
> *says the Teacher.*
> *"Utterly meaningless!*
> *Everything is meaningless." (1:2)*

The Running Theme

"Meaningless"! The word is repeated again and again. And in Hebrew idiom it becomes a superlative form of expression: "vanity of vanities." What does the word mean?

The Hebrew word that is the challenging heartbeat of Ecclesiastes is *hebel*. It means a vapor, a puff of breath, a whiff of smoke, a passing cloud, a swirl of steam. So it is a very suggestive word for a variety of metaphorical uses. In different contexts it can have slightly different senses and flavors:

1. **Empty**, pointless, of no benefit at all. That was the older meaning of the word "vanity"—as in the KJV translation. Something that might seem very attractive in itself but in the end proves to be just a waste of time and effort, not worth anything at all. "As useless as a chocolate teapot," as they say in the northeast of England.

2. **Transient**, insubstantial, fleeting, not having any permanence or duration. It may look wonderful and magnificent, but it all disappears very quickly and nothing is left. Like the morning dew or mist, or steam from a boiling kettle.

3. **Deceptive**, false, not what it's cracked up to be (the word is used about idols in that sense). Something you shouldn't bother to believe in because it will always disappoint you. "Scotch mist" is another British idiom that means something that barely exists, or you are just imagining, and you'd waste your time looking for it.

4. **Frustrating**, something you can never get hold of or grasp fully—like the wind. You can chase it all you like but never catch it or hold it in your hands. "Like herding cats," as the saying goes.

5. **Absurd**, something that seems wildly unreasonable and illogical, making no sense in relation to other known facts or truths.

6. **Baffling**, enigmatic. You know there must be some meaning or point in life, but it constantly eludes you; you can't get to the bottom of it. In the end life is a mystery, an enigma. Whatever meaning there is (and presumably there is one) is hidden from us. We just struggle to make sense of things that seem senseless most of the time.

I think the author of Ecclesiastes oscillates mostly between the first and the last two (though sometimes the flavor of the others can be tasted too). That is, sometimes he sounds downright pessimistic:

life has no meaning at all; it's all completely pointless. Get over it! That's the flavor of the NIV's "meaningless."

But at other times he sounds just genuinely baffled. He seems to be saying, "I know life is better than death. I know wisdom is better than folly. I know hard work is better than being lazy. I believe those things and I believe in the God who made them so and gives us life to enjoy. But I just can't find out any reason *why* those things are that way. And to be honest, so much in life actually seems to turn them upside down. Life is just one big puzzle. It baffles me, even though I have tried every possible way to explore it and make sense of it. Life itself remains an enigma."

I think you'll find that if you read in the word "baffling" when you come across the word "meaningless" in our English translations, like the NIV, it often helps to capture the likely meaning of what the author is getting at. Or sometimes the words "pointless" or "absurd" will sound right.

This sense of "a baffling enigma" seems close to Qoheleth's view of life in this world as we know it. We live in a world we just can't understand. Or at least, even though there is a great and increasing amount that we *can and do* understand, there are aspects of life and our experience that just don't make sense and so much that seems beyond our abilities or our control. And even when we have an intuitive belief that there must be a point and a meaning in it all somehow, we can't quite put our finger on it with definitive and satisfying answers. That is what propels Qoheleth on his journey.

The Key Question

What do people gain from all their labors
at which they toil under the sun? (1:3)

This is the programmatic question that governs the book and its search. The question is repeated at 2:22, 3:9, and 5:16.

The word "gain" means "profit" or "benefit." So the question is, What's the payoff for a lifetime of work? What do you get in the end? What are you left with? What is the positive gain from all your efforts?

The word "labors" is somewhat negative. It is not the ordinary Hebrew word for work but instead reeks of toil and sweat. And that, of course, is what our human world of work became after Genesis 3. We sweat just to eat bread. We toil on the soil to wrest our food from it. We *have to work* just to survive in this fallen world, and that kind of work is pretty hard.

But, on the other hand, work is a good thing in itself (as Qoheleth will agree again and again). God created us in God's own image, and the first picture of God we see in the Bible is as a worker: thinking, deciding, planning, executing, shaping, forming, filling, accomplishing in a systematic and purposeful way. A creature that will reflect God in some way simply has to have similar capacities. And we do. It is fundamentally and constitutionally human to work. Work is an essential dimension of our God-imaging role within creation.

It is by our work that we participate in human society. It is by our work that we make our lives useful to others, and of course we gain from the work of others in return. That is what human civilization is all about—this great human project of shared work and the shared benefits of everybody else's work. Work is itself *part* of the meaning of human life (though we'll see a lot of problems with work in chapter 3). That is why to be *unable* to work, or to be *deprived* of work, or to *refuse* to work—are all conditions that reduce our humanity. Enforced or voluntary idleness are alike dehumanizing to some degree. And of course, we are not here equating "work" exclusively with "employment," even if they often overlap. People work in all kinds of ways for which they do not get paid in financial terms (ask any mother).

So the question in verse 3, though it focuses on human *work*, is probably asking at a deeper level about human *life*, since we have to work to live. But at the end of it all, asks our author, What is the profit? Where is the gain? What is the point of even a whole lifetime of work? When you get to the end of your life, and all your life's work, will it all have been worth anything in the great scheme of things?

Well, you might think that verse 2 has already answered the question of verse 3! It's obvious! There's no gain at all when you count it all up. It's all just meaningless, and I'm going to prove it to you, says Qoheleth, and in the end you'll die anyway. . . .

But hold on. The journey has just started. The question becomes the quest. We have just begun the long search that will go on through the whole book. Is verse 2 really *all* we can say? Is that the *whole* truth about human life?

Well, let's see. . . .

It's worth just pausing to check what that phrase ". . . *under the sun*" means. It comes here in verse 3 and will occur twenty-nine times altogether in the book. There has been a line of interpretation that takes it to imply, "life on this earth *without reference to God*." The assumption is that God is "up in heaven above the sun" while we are "down here on earth under the sun." So Ecclesiastes is telling us that we really ought to be concerned about life up in heaven ("above the sun") and leave behind all this obsession with earthly things ("under the sun").

But I think this is probably not what the author means by that phrase. He does *not* deliberately exclude God from his reflections. On the contrary, he *does* bring God into his discussion quite often. God is very much involved and active in life "under the sun," though that seems to add to, rather than solve, his problems. The author is neither an actual atheist, nor is he pretending to be one— that is, voicing the atheist's complaints and then opposing them with a more spiritual message.

The phrase "under the sun" is probably meant simply as a kind of inclusive or comprehensive framework: "everywhere on earth the sun shines." It may be similar to the way we use the words "on earth" to express some hypothetically universal context for an emphatic question. "What on earth do you think you're doing?" "Where on earth are you going?" "Why on earth did she do that?"

Similarly, by his repeated expression "under the sun," our author seems to be saying, "No matter where you look on the earth, this is the kind of thing you'll find. This is the whole of human life and experience as we live it from day to day under the light of the sun." It is a way of making assertions that he thinks are universally true—even though some of them are contradictory and most are baffling!

THE CIRCULARITY OF LIFE (1:4–11)

The Frame-Narrator now steps in to offer an initial justification for his opening challenging assertion and question. This will line us up for the full exploration that will follow in Qoheleth's auto-biographical quest, after he is introduced to us at verse 12.

Here we have the first of several "poems" in the book. Of course, a lot of the book is written in a kind of poetic verse. But there are some self-contained poetic passages like this that stand out as short, coherent poems in their own right. This one expands upon what he means by his bald exclamation in verse 2.

> ⁴*Generations come and generations go,*
>   *but the earth remains forever.*
> ⁵*The sun rises and the sun sets,*
>   *and hurries back to where it rises.*
> ⁶*The wind blows to the south*
>   *and turns to the north;*
> *round and round it goes,*
>   *ever returning on its course.*
> ⁷*All streams flow into the sea,*
>   *yet the sea is never full.*
> *To the place the streams come from,*

there they return again.
⁸All things are wearisome,
*   more than one can say.*
The eye never has enough of seeing,
*   nor the ear its fill of hearing.*
⁹What has been will be again,
*   what has been done will be done again;*
*   there is nothing new under the sun.*
¹⁰Is there anything of which one can say,
*   "Look! This is something new"?*
It was here already, long ago;
*   it was here before our time.*
¹¹No one remembers the former generations,
*   and even those yet to come*
will not be remembered
*   by those who follow them.*

The poem has an interesting concentric or chiastic structure[1]:

A. *(v. 4). Human life (even generations of it) is pretty fleeting and insignificant in comparison to the enduring ages of the earth. Elsewhere, the ancient age of the earth is a matter of reassurance and praise to God. Here it simply highlights the transience of human life, perhaps drawing on Psalm 90, where the same point is emphasized.*
  B. *(vv. 5–6). Everything in nature just goes round and round. Elsewhere, the daily rising of the sun is a matter of thanksgiving and a metaphor for dependability. Here it is seen merely as a boring repetition.*
    C. *(vv. 7–8). So nothing ever gets filled up and finished. Therefore, even though our search with our eyes and ears is insatiable and never-ending, we will never get a*

---

1. A chiastic or concentric structure is one where the author makes a series of points in order, "on the way in," arrives at the central point, and then repeats the same points in reverse order "on the way out." Thus, A, B, C, B', A'.

satisfactory answer to the meaning of life and the problems it poses for us. We just end up exhausted trying.

B'. *(vv. 9–10). Everything in history just goes round and round too. Elsewhere, biblical writers discerned patterns in history as pointing to the dependable character of Yahweh—the God who can and will "do again" what he has done before but who can also do astonishing new things. Here history is reduced to endless circularity where nothing is new, but merely repeated.*

A'. *(v. 11). And anyway, you won't last long enough—everyone gets forgotten in the end. Human history is one long, dark, black hole.*

So the main point comes in the middle (vv. 7–8), and the outer circles make supporting points. We are going to join Qoheleth on a great search to answer the question of verse 3, says the author, but get ready to be worn out with frustration. It's a search that will take you round and round and round again like the wind, but you'll be no nearer to a satisfactory answer to all your questions, any more than the sea gets finally filled up by the rivers. The message of the poem is the same as its structure—circular. Everything just goes around and nothing is ever settled and final. That's the central point in verses 7–8.

There are two major flaws in his case, however.

First of all, if he is going to explore by "eyes and ears" only (that is, by empirical observation alone), then yes, he is doomed to frustration. If he plans to judge everything only by what he observes and in that way make himself the sole judge of fact and truth—then yes, his observations will lead eventually to the frustrating verdict of *hebel*. His perspective will be relentlessly subjective and constantly open to contradiction and deconstruction. He will see one thing and then see the exact opposite and find it impossible to bridge the gap between them. And that is exactly what we will find happening again and again all through the book. There will be constant baffling tensions between what he knows and what he sees. The observations of his eyes and ears alone will never by themselves answer the deepest questions or solve the riddles of the universe.

And secondly, he is already out of line with a key biblical insight and truth. For according to God's revelation in the prophetic Scriptures, history is *not* circular or cyclical. History is not like nature, with its perennial round of seasons. History is being governed by God. History is the outworking of God's own plan and purpose. God is at work within history to fulfill his promise. History, according to the Bible, is God's Story (e.g., Isa 40:22–24; 41:21–29; Jer 18:7–10; Pss 33:10–11; 96:4–10).

Israel knew that. Qoheleth, as someone who knew and shared Israel's faith, should have known that too. But by excluding it here, at the very start of his quest, he cuts himself off from some vital parts of God's revelation in history—and we'll have to come back to that point later.

A cyclical view of history will always end up being hopeless. The reason for that is simple. A circular or cyclical view of history lacks two things. First, it lacks a sense of *purpose* (theologians call that "teleology")—a goal toward which things are moving. If you are just going round in circles, you are not "going anywhere." No wonder it feels meaningless! And second, it lacks a sense of an *end* (theologians call that "eschatology")—that God will ultimately "finish the story," complete his purposes, and achieve the total fulfilment of his promises, so there is a future to be eagerly anticipated. And with neither purpose nor end, there can be no real hope. And that is exactly what Qoheleth finds. That is why he ends up so frustrated and (almost) in complete despair.

AN EXPLORATION OF LIFE (1:12–2:11)

Qoheleth now introduces himself and sets off on his quest. He repeats the *persona* that the Frame-Narrator gave him in verse 1. Qoheleth is a leader of people (his name or title probably means that); he is a believer in God; he is endowed with wisdom (educated);

and he imagines that he has been provided with all the resources anybody could ever assemble for his quest. He pictures himself with all the wisdom, wealth, and opportunity that a King Solomon could muster.

> *12I, the Teacher, was king over Israel in Jerusalem. 13I applied my mind to study and to explore by wisdom all that is done under the heavens. What a heavy burden God has laid on mankind! 14I have seen all the things that are done under the sun; all of them are meaningless, a chasing after the wind.*
>
> *15What is crooked cannot be straightened;*
>   *what is lacking cannot be counted. (1:12–15)*

Qoheleth sets himself a huge project of exploration—"All that is done under the heavens" (v. 13)—probably not quite the kind of research topic that would be accepted for a PhD proposal today. This guy is ambitious.

And he is also dead serious. "I applied my mind. . . ." In Hebrew, that is, "I gave my heart." And in Hebrew, the heart is the seat, not so much of our emotions, as of our intellect, choices, and will. So this is a very strong statement of intention. He is going to do some purposeful hard thinking. He's going to put in some really demanding intellectual effort. And that is good, of course; we were created in the image of God with astonishing capacity for rational thought and problem solving. But it's also risky, if he is going to depend only on what his "mind" tells him through his eyes and ears. As we said above—if his whole project is based on purely empirical observation and deduction, this will be a bumpy ride.

He adds that he will pursue this project "by wisdom"—and he says that repeatedly in the coming sections (e.g., 2:3, 9, 12, 7:23–29; 8:16). And of course, that also sounds good. But at this stage his wisdom is totally self-referential—*I* saw, *I* thought, etc. It is not until the very end of the book, and only in the epilogue of the

Frame-Narrator, that we find the essential affirmation of Proverbs, that the very beginning and first principle of wisdom is the fear of the Lord, so that we submit all our thinking and acting to him, as the essence of wisdom (12:13, cf. Prov 1:7). Again, Qoheleth must have known about this governing principle of biblical wisdom. But it does not appear to be his starting point here. No, Qoheleth is going to do his exploration by observation only.

And, like many a PhD student, he affirms his initial conclusion right up front—leaving us to hope that he will provide adequate argumentation to support the conclusion later. And so he states his immediate and preliminary negative observation in verses 13b–15.

"What a heavy burden" (NIV), in Hebrew, is: "It is an *evil* (*ra'*) business or task." This is an astonishingly bleak assessment (which probably finds an echo in many a PhD student's heart at the start of their project). After all, we know (as the author did) that God created the world "good" and that work itself is a good thing—which Qoheleth will praise repeatedly later on, as we shall see. Yet here he pronounces the whole human enterprise "bad"—*and he blames God!* It is God who has "given" this heavy, evil, "unhappy business" (ESV) to humanity. It is God who lays this burden of frustrating, meaningless work on our shoulders.

Immediately then, we can see that he is not excluding God from his research or equations. God is very much involved in all the processes, events, situations, and outcomes that he will explore. But far from that conviction *solving* anything, he can only conclude that God is somehow implicated in the way human life is such a heavy burden and all human accomplishments seem to be ultimately as frustrating as chasing the wind (v. 14). It's all God's fault!

Now if the apostle Paul were able to chip in at this point, I think he would agree! But he would do so with a wink and a smile. For Paul would say that although evil and frustration were not God's original intention for creation and humanity, it was indeed God himself who "subjected" the creation to futility and frustration in response to our wicked rebellion against God. *But*, Paul would continue with a smile (knowing more than Qoheleth), because of the death and resurrection of Jesus Christ, creation and humanity together have *hope* (Rom 8:18–25).

So, as we shall see at several points on the way through this book, Qoheleth insists that God is somehow involved in all the baffling and frustrating aspects of life on earth (e.g., 3:9–11,18; 6:1–2; 7:13–14; 9:1). And while this sounds so negative, it does conceal a positive truth. Life in all its absurdity and unfairness is *still under the sovereign control of God.*

And that gives us the quiet reassurance that, if *hebel* was not God's first word about creation, it need not be his last.

But Qoheleth is in no mood to take all that on board right now. For him, an old-fashioned proverb seems undeniable. Verse 15 makes the flat assertion that there is something radically bent about the world and there's nothing we can do to fix it. Hard to disagree.

Nevertheless, that initial assessment is not going to stop him from trying to find *something* in life that will give it some meaningful purpose and value. So he throws himself into his great research project. He recounts to us how he explored at least four ways to find meaning and fulfillment in life.

Academic Learning

> *16I said to myself, "Look, I have increased in wisdom more than anyone who has ruled over Jerusalem before me; I have experienced much of wisdom and knowledge." 17Then I applied myself to the understanding of wisdom, and also of madness and folly, but I learned that this, too, is a chasing after the wind.*

> *18For with much wisdom comes much sorrow;*
> *the more knowledge, the more grief. (1:16–18)*

He begins well, or so it seems. He begins in the way all of us who are parents encourage our children: Get educated! Study hard! Well, he does that, and he works through all the grades and the degrees and excels in every subject. He attains great wisdom and great discernment between what constitutes true wisdom and what is mere "madness and folly" (which is not entirely lacking in academic circles). He gets that PhD. He becomes what we might call an elite intellectual. A professor. A consultant. A government advisor. There is nothing wrong with this. Wisdom is highly commended in Scripture. Education is a good and desirable thing.

But his great learning didn't satisfy or answer the deepest questions of life. It was a fruitless search. And a painful one in the end. He discovered the ironic truth of the common saying that "ignorance is bliss." He would have been happier if he hadn't learned so much, for it seems that "the more you know, the more it hurts" (v. 18; GNT).

Hedonism

> [1] *I said to myself, "Come now, I will test you with pleasure to find out what is good." But that also proved to be meaningless.* [2] *"Laughter," I said, "is madness. And what does pleasure accomplish?" (2:1–2)*

So, like many a first-year student in the rush of intoxicating freedom, he throws himself into the pursuit of pleasure. He has fun. Doubtless he enjoys the easy life of a fun-loving crowd of friends. They have a great time and laugh a lot together.

And again, we can't complain too much. God gave us life to enjoy, and even the great sea creatures have fun playing in the ocean (and perhaps so does God himself, frolicking around with them, according to a very plausible reading of Ps 104:26; see ESV footnote). Even Wisdom itself is portrayed as full of delight and joy in the creation of the world (Prov 8:30). So we don't need to frown on his pleasure and laughter as something sinful in itself.

Are pleasure and laughter "good" (v. 1)? Well, in and of themselves, we would have to say yes. They are part of God's good gift in creation. Of course, they can be perverted by sin—such as taking pleasure in cruel behavior, laughing at the poor or disabled.

But there is no indication that Qoheleth's pleasure and laughter were tainted in that way. We may assume that he just allowed himself to have an innocently good time. Good for him, then.

But the relentless question returns: What did the pursuit of pleasure accomplish? Nothing. What does the memory of helpless laughter sound like after you stop? Madness. Pleasure by itself is a poor contender for the ultimate meaning of life.

Controlled Folly

I tried cheering myself with wine, and embracing folly—my mind still guiding me with wisdom. I wanted to see what was good for people to do under the heavens during the few days of their lives. (2:3)

Qoheleth now swings to the opposite of his first experiment in academic wisdom. He throws himself into the world of irrational folly, with the aid of wine. If being sober and learned brought no satisfaction, what about being drunk and stupid? Could that make any better sense of life? It's a curious decision, but remember (to our relief), this is just his story, not his recommendation.

"Embracing folly," he says. It sounds pretty modern. Indeed, one could say this is a perceptively accurate insight into the increasingly dominant character of Western culture. We combine a cult of empty celebrity (being famous just for being famous—not for actually accomplishing anything of value) with derisory rejection of the wisdom or advice of those who actually do know something, whether academic, scientific, economic, or from a lifetime of skilled practice. The "democratizing" of knowledge through the internet elevates anybody's tweeted opinion to the same status of validity as a carefully researched and evidence-based medical paper.

Perhaps the COVID-19 pandemic has restored some degree of faith in the "wisdom" of scientific skills and expertise, as we have witnessed the incredible ability to do genomic sequencing of the virus and its variants and to produce effective vaccines so quickly.

And yet, equally incredibly, the "folly" of conspiracy theories, anti-vax rhetoric and social media, extreme forms of "faith and healing" spiritualities, anti-science prejudice, and sheer distrust of "experts" are rampant in many countries and cultures—from presidents to people on the street. "Embracing folly" is putting it mildly.

Ironically, Qoheleth tells us he embraced *folly* while letting his mind still be guided by *wisdom*. It seems that he allowed himself to experience depths of inebriation and mental dissolution—while still somehow observing himself with some kind of analytical reflection on the experience. We can question the prudence of such an attempt. Can you really allow yourself to get blind drunk and idiotic and trust your poor brain to observe it rationally? But there is a deeper irony than the obvious risks. For when he says, "my mind still guiding me *with wisdom*," we have to ask, "What wisdom? Whose wisdom?" Certainly not the wisdom of Proverbs. The warnings of Proverbs against the temptations and dangers of drunkenness are stark.

> [23:19]Listen, my son, and be wise,
>> and set your heart on the right path:
> [20]Do not join those who drink too much wine
>> or gorge themselves on meat,
> [21]for drunkards and gluttons become poor,
>> and drowsiness clothes them in rags. . . .
> [29]Who has woe? Who has sorrow?
>> Who has strife? Who has complaints?
>> Who has needless bruises? Who has bloodshot eyes?
> [30]Those who linger over wine,
>> who go to sample bowls of mixed wine.
> [31]Do not gaze at wine when it is red,
>> when it sparkles in the cup,
>> when it goes down smoothly!
> [32]In the end it bites like a snake
>> and poisons like a viper.

> [33]Your eyes will see strange sights,
>   and your mind will imagine confusing things.
> [34]You will be like one sleeping on the high seas,
>   lying on top of the rigging.
> [35]"They hit me," you will say, "but I'm not hurt!
>   They beat me, but I don't feel it!
> When will I wake up
>   so I can find another drink?" (Prov 23:19–21, 29–35)

And even more significantly, since Qoheleth is imagining himself as a king:

> [4]It is not for kings, Lemuel—
>   it is not for kings to drink wine,
>   not for rulers to crave beer,
> [5]lest they drink and forget what has been decreed,
>   and deprive all the oppressed of their rights.
>   (Prov 31:4–5)

In light of such texts, whatever "wisdom" Qoheleth claims is guiding him, it is certainly not the wisdom that comes from the fear of the Lord and submission to his word. So we are hardly surprised that he does not even bother to give any verdict on this particular experiment. If he was sincerely trying "to see what was *good* for people," this wasn't it (as he surely should have known!).

Productive Work

Sober and sensible again, he throws himself into constructive projects—as Solomon had done. Here at last is something promising. Here is something productive, beneficial to himself and others. Won't this bring a fulfilling and satisfying answer to his search?

[4]I undertook great projects: I built houses for myself and planted vineyards. [5]I made gardens and parks and planted all kinds of

*fruit trees in them. ⁶I made reservoirs to water groves of flourishing
trees. ⁷I bought male and female slaves and had other slaves who
were born in my house. I also owned more herds and flocks than
anyone in Jerusalem before me. ⁸I amassed silver and gold for
myself, and the treasure of kings and provinces. I acquired male
and female singers, and a harem as well—the delights of a man's
heart. ⁹I became greater by far than anyone in Jerusalem before
me. In all this my wisdom stayed with me.*

> *¹⁰I denied myself nothing my eyes desired;*
> *   I refused my heart no pleasure.*
> *My heart took delight in all my labor,*
> *   and this was the reward for all my toil.*
> *¹¹Yet when I surveyed all that my hands had done*
> *   and what I had toiled to achieve,*
> *everything was meaningless, a chasing after the wind;*
> *   nothing was gained under the sun. (2:4–11)*

Now most of what he describes here can be applauded as good
and commendable (well, not the slave trade and the harem! But this
is an imagined ancient Near Eastern king). Indeed, there are some
clear echoes of the creation stories of Genesis 1–2 in the way he
describes his accomplishments. There is productive work: gardens,
fruitful trees, watercourses. He is a wealth creator. He provides
employment. He loves horticulture and develops agriculture. He
patronizes music and choirs. Maybe it all sounds a bit boastful, and
certainly it has a strongly self-centered flavor, but it is at least more
deserving of the "wisdom" label than his previous drunken foray
(v. 3). These were good and worthy things to do. They still are.

And it was great! Verse 10 is a hearty celebration of the joys
of work—*while he was doing it*. He took delight in all his projects,
and that was his reward. And again, we have to agree that this
can be very true. For don't we often find that there is an *intrinsic*
reward in doing a good job well? We get absorbed in a demanding

project, we get busy, we draw on the stuff we know well, we deploy all our gifts and training, we expend great effort, we organize and cooperate with colleagues, we relish the pressure and deadlines, we solve the problems and overcome the difficulties, we are satisfied with the steady progress, we keep the goal in mind, we focus and prioritize, we sacrifice other things and discipline our time, *we get the job done*—and we feel good about it (most of the time). It can be very fulfilling. "This is what I was made for," we might think, even in exhaustion at the end of a busy day.

And there is something creationally good about this too, something uniquely human, for it is the outworking of being made in the image of God. And Qoheleth will want to tell us later, and often, that the sheer ability to work is in itself a good and God-given thing (e.g., 2:24; 3:13, 22; 5:18). So it's not surprising that he enjoyed it all *while he was doing it*.

But that is where the comparison with God falls short. For when God "stood back" and "surveyed" all that his hands had made, he saw and pronounced it "good, very good" (see the sevenfold repetition of the word "good" from Gen 1:4–31) God was completely satisfied not only in the "doing" of creation, but in the end result. After all his "doing," God could bless and hallow and enjoy Sabbath rest.

But not Qoheleth. Verse 11 is a devastating concluding verdict. Unlike God, he says, "when I surveyed all that my hands had done" (which was phenomenal), he could find no lasting value or ultimate meaning in it all. In a moment he will give us some reasons for this negativity. But right now, it stands as a testimony of utter disillusionment. "And behold," he seems to say, "the whole lot was *hebel*." And if that was so, had it all been worth it? The work itself was great while it lasted—even if it lasted for a lifetime. But the very essence and meaning of life was still as much an enigma as before he started.

The question of 1:3 remains unanswered.

The assertion of 1:2 stands.

HATING LIFE! (2:12–23)

"Then I turned . . ." he says (v. 12). Qoheleth has a change of focus as he reflects on his experiments and observations. He has explored the heights of what he considers to be wisdom and sunk to the depths of madness and folly. He has done all he can. Nobody could do more than "Solomon"!

> [12] *Then I turned my thoughts to consider wisdom,*
> *and also madness and folly.*
> *What more can the king's successor do*
> *than what has already been done?*
> [13] *I saw that wisdom is better than folly,*
> *just as light is better than darkness.*
> [14] *The wise have eyes in their heads,*
> *while the fool walks in the darkness; (2:12–14a)*

So, on the one hand, he reminds himself of the standard response—what everybody knows. There is a "received wisdom" that everybody learns from their parents, or at school, or in the Boy Scouts. Verses 13–14a make a very straightforward binary affirmation. Wisdom is better than folly, as light is better than darkness. It's standard stuff from the book of Proverbs. He even has the right quotes. Verse 14a is the kind of proverb your grandmother would come out with, "for your own good," till you're tired of hearing it.

But then, on the other hand, he swivels to completely subvert what he has just quoted: "but I came to realize. . . ." This is the first example of some typical tactics of this author, so we'd better get used to them. He has just told us *what he knows to be true* and then without a break, he tells us why *it makes no sense* or doesn't matter in the end.

> [14b] *but I came to realize*
> *that the same fate overtakes them both.*

¹⁵Then I said to myself,

> *"The fate of the fool will overtake me also.*
> * What then do I gain by being wise?"*
> *I said to myself,*
> * "This too is meaningless."*
> *¹⁶For the wise, like the fool, will not be long remembered;*
> * the days have already come when both have been*
> *   forgotten.*
> *Like the fool, the wise too must die! (2:14b–16)*

He has crashed out of the world he thought he did understand, the world of accepted truths, into the world he can't understand. And the crash will go on echoing through the book as he struggles to find a way to reconcile the two.

For even if you agree with the conventional truths of verses 13–14a (and who wouldn't?), you come up against two apparently unanswerable problems: death and legacy (or the lack of it).

Death (v. 15)

Here comes the great equalizer. What's the point of being wise if you end up just as dead as a fool? This is a gloomy thought that he will come back to several times, with increasing pessimism (e.g., 3:19–21; 5:15–17; 9:1–6). He gets it in early here. Somehow Genesis 3 trumps whatever benefit he can see from living in the world of Genesis 1–2. We all end up dead in the end.

Qoheleth can't see anything beyond death. And the Old Testament Scriptures did not reveal much about that either, so we may excuse him a little. And yet, for some Israelites the promises of God gave them hope that the righteous would not ultimately be abandoned to the same fate as the wicked. Somehow it seemed inconceivable that a believer's relationship with God, shaped by a lifetime of faith, love, and obedience, should simply be snuffed out entirely at death. Psalm 16:9–11 suggest such a hope. But Qoheleth isn't paying much attention to the Scriptures here. All he allows himself to use are his observation and his reason, and by themselves they can't penetrate beyond death. And as far as he can see, death sucks all the value out of being wise, or anything else for that matter.

Legacy (v. 16)

No matter how wise you become in this life, you won't be remembered for very long after you're dead, any more than the fool will be. So stop dreaming of some wonderful legacy that will make your life worthwhile. In the end, time will dissolve your memory just as much as the earth will dissolve your remains.

Once again, it is possible Qoheleth is deliberately questioning a standard piece of the wisdom of Proverbs.

> The memory of the righteous will be a blessing [or the
> name of the righteous is used in blessings,
> (NIV)],
> **But the name of the wicked will rot**.
> (Prov 10:7; my emphasis)

Sorry, says Qoheleth, that's only half true. The fact is, we'll all rot, and sooner or later, we'll all be forgotten. Get over it.

That leads him to an outburst of deeply felt emotion. He cannot bear this frustrating inability to find value or meaning in life—even with all his best efforts. So he targets life itself.

[17] So I hated life, because the work that is done under the sun was grievous to me. All of it is meaningless, a chasing after the wind. [18] I hated all the things I had toiled for under the sun, because I must leave them to the one who comes after me. [19] And who knows whether that person will be wise or foolish? Yet they will have control over all the fruit of my toil into which I have poured my effort and skill under the sun. This too is meaningless. [20] So my

heart began to despair over all my toilsome labor under the sun.
21 For a person may labor with wisdom, knowledge and skill, and
then they must leave all they own to another who has not toiled
for it. This too is meaningless and a great misfortune. (2:17–21)

And on top of the frustration of his own life, he imagines with bitter sarcasm what might well happen after his death, in spite of all his hard work and accomplishments. For you can work hard all your life, do a lot of good, and build up a whole business empire, but you have no control over what happens when you die. Your successor may be an idiot who squanders it all and who didn't work for it or deserve it in the first place! And where's the sense in that? None at all that he can see.

And indeed, that *would* be the ultimate horizon of hopelessness if all we had was this life with no hope for any future beyond our personal death. It will take the rest of the Bible's story to provide that hope and to assure us that what we will have done in this life counts for eternity in the new creation. Ultimately it will take the resurrection of Christ to convince us that "our labor in the Lord is not in vain" (1 Cor 15:58). But Qoheleth could have no inkling of that yet.

So in verse 22 he comes back again to his programmatic question, the one he asked in 1:3.

What do people get for all the toil and anxious striving with which
they labor under the sun? (2:22)

And in verse 23 he answers it.

All their days their work is grief and pain; even at night their minds
do not rest. This too is meaningless. (2:23)

What do we get? Nothing but sleeplessness and despair—until our days are over. Qoheleth would be inclined to agree with the famous graffito,

Life sucks. Then you die.

Indeed, Qoheleth could justifiably claim to have inspired that bleak summary of life's pointlessness. It gets Qoheleth's most pessimistic observations down to five words.

LOVING LIFE! (2:24–26)

Then comes a complete shock! He gives us no warning. He doesn't raise a hand for a rhetorical pause, as if to say, "But having said that, let me also add. . . ." He doesn't say, "On the other hand . . . ," or, "Nevertheless. . . ." He doesn't smile encouragingly: "Let's all cheer up a bit here."

Qoheleth just switches gears and makes this bold statement about the goodness of life and work, seen as a wonderful gift from the hand of God. The contrast with verses 17–23 is stark and tense.

> [24]*A person can do nothing better than to eat and drink and find satisfaction in their own toil. This too, I see, is from the hand of God,* [25]*for without him, who can eat or find enjoyment?* [26]*To the person who pleases him, God gives wisdom, knowledge and happiness, but to the sinner he gives the task of gathering and storing up wealth to hand it over to the one who pleases God.*[2] *This too is meaningless, a chasing after the wind.* (2:24–26)

This is the first of seven places in the book of Ecclesiastes[3] where such a positive view of life is expressed—with increasing

---

2. This rather enigmatic verse probably makes most sense seen as a counterpoint to verses 14b-15. The implication of those verses could be that there is ultimately no difference between wisdom and folly, between good and evil, since death eliminates all distinctions. Verse 26 retorts that *God* preserves the distinctions. God knows those who please him and those who don't, and will act towards each appropriately. There is a moral distinction in the universe and God will uphold it. The verse is not a mandate for forcible redistribution of the property of sinners to the righteous—for only God has the prerogative and the discernment to exercise such judgment.

3. See also 3:12–14, 22; 5:18–20; 8:15; 9:7–10; 11:7–10.

elaboration. They are sometimes called the *carpe diem* texts. Seize the moment! Life is good! Enjoy it now while you can! Relish the good things God has given us.

Now we need to be careful how we hear his phrase "nothing better." It might sound very negative or cynical. In colloquial English we use the expression "nothing better" in a way that expresses harsh criticism. We might complain to the waiter in a restaurant, "This meal is rubbish; have you got *nothing better* to give me?" Or a frustrated parent pleads with a lazy, time-wasting child, "Have you *nothing better* to do than lie there all day?" In that vein, we might think Qoheleth is saying, "You might as well enjoy eating, drinking, and working, because, even though it's a miserable load of rubbish, it's the best there is in this life. It's pretty insignificant, but there's nothing better. Get over it." That kind of cynicism is not how the Hebrew would have been heard.

Nor should we take these verses as a kind of hedonistic shrug: "Life is a complete waste of time—so we might as well just eat, drink, and be merry, for tomorrow we die." That is, just give in to unbridled pleasure-seeking in the face of the frustrations of life. But he's already tried that and knows it was an empty charade.

No, it seems that Qoheleth is doing here what he will do again and again. He is stating his *alternative answer* to the key question of 1:3. We know what his *predominant answer* is—that is clear throughout the book: life is *hebel*, baffling and enigmatic. But he cannot get away from the foundational truths of his Israelite scriptural faith. He may not understand a lot about life in this world, but he still understands this, because it is axiomatic to his very identity as an Israelite: life is good, because it comes from the good God our Creator.

Yes, of course, we have to live with the dismal and debilitating consequences of Genesis 3—curse, frustration, death, futility. *But Genesis 1 and 2 still count.* Those chapters, and other Scriptures that build on them, still constitute the underlying foundation of life on this earth. It is God who has given us life, food, wine, work—*and it is right and proper to enjoy them to the full.* To do otherwise would be to throw God's good gifts back in his face. That would *not* be good. What *is* good is to take these gifts from God's hand and enjoy them.

It is noticeable that God is completely absent from the whole section of 1:12–2:23 (apart from the barbed accusation of 1:13). Qoheleth was relying solely on his observations and experiments, guided by his own (questionable) wisdom. Whereas, in significant contrast, God is completely central to 2:24–26. So Qoheleth accepts that God has created us to live and work in his good creation, and it is both a duty and a joy to respond to God in appropriately grateful and affirmative living.

However, it would be wrong, I think, to imagine that Qoheleth is engaged in some kind of self-correcting ventriloquism. That is, it is not that he first of all *imagines* somebody saying all the negative stuff about life *without God*, and then he piously corrects them with a cheerful, "But if you bring God into the picture, everything makes sense and you can be happy and content after all." He is not as naively simplistic as that. For the point he will make as we go along (and makes it right at the end of v. 26) is that *even when you do bring God into the picture, life still doesn't make a lot of sense some of the time.* As I said before, for Qoheleth God is not the simple solution to all his problems. If anything, it is his faith in the reality and sovereignty of God that makes his struggles worse. That's the trouble with biblical monotheism, you see. Knowing there is one sovereign living God is itself part of the problem!

This is not a battle between atheism and faith. It is a battle *within* faith itself. It is the battle between what is known and believed to be good and true, and what is observed to be meaningless and baffling, in the world God created, rules over, and has put us in.

Qoheleth is struggling with the *God* he doesn't understand *and* with the *world* he doesn't understand. Trying to put it all together simply baffles him—it comes to *hebel* in the end—as far as he can see.

So a huge chasm is opened up. Can you see and feel it as we come to the end of this first leg of his long journey?

On the one side of the chasm, there is the apparently meaningless, baffling enigma of life—all the unanswerable questions that life throws up. No matter how hard you work or how clever you are, it all ends in death.

But on the other side of the chasm is the sheer goodness and joy of life in God's creation, when accepted joyfully from the hand of God. But even as we relish the wonderful joy of life, food, drink, work, marriage, etc., it only throws into even deeper, jarring contrast the brokenness, pain, and unfairness of what we see around us. Faith and observation seem poles apart. Yet the author just puts them side by side.

First verses 22–23.

Then verses 24–25.

And a chasm in between.

How can this chasm be bridged? Is there anything he or we can put in place that might reconcile these contradictory perspectives on life? Can they both be true? Or will one of them have to win in the end? We have quite a journey ahead, for Qoheleth's quest is only just begun.

Perhaps these are the sort of questions you struggle with also. Perhaps they are questions that you get asked by others who are amazed that you persevere in being a person of faith when so much in the world seems to contradict what you believe. Remember that Qoheleth too was a person of faith.

And here's the thing: Having faith does not mean *not* having questions. And equally, having faith does *not* mean having nice, easy answers to those questions.

But for the moment, let's travel on with Qoheleth, striving to see things from his point of view, to walk in his sandals, and to hear him out until we get to the end of his quest.

QUESTIONS FOR REFLECTION
AND DISCUSSION

1. Have you ever been asked (or asked yourself) the key question of 1:3? What sort of answers have you come up with? Why does the question matter?

2. Discuss the different ways that Qoheleth tried (and failed) to find meaning and satisfaction in life in 1:16–2:11. What are the modern equivalents of these? And what others would you add that people try today? Why do they not provide any ultimate meaning for life?

3. There is a tension between Qoheleth's *emotions* in 2:17–18 and his *convictions* in 2:24–25. Do you ever feel the same tension? Do you know people who express the same kind of tension or confusion? How can we live with it?

MYSTERIES OF TIME AND INJUSTICE

Ecclesiastes 3:1–4:3

Qoheleth has had a busy time in the quest he describes in the first two chapters of the book. So now he turns from all that very specific exploration of life and work and all his intensive projects to a much broader, more philosophical reflection on the rhythms of life in general. He reflects on our experience of life in this world of time and our intuitions that there must be something beyond time. What is the meaning of it all?

He launches this part of his journey with another poem—the second in his book.

THE RIDDLE OF TIME AND ETERNITY (3:1–15)

> *¹There is a time for everything,*
> *and a season for every activity under the heavens:*
>
> *²a time to be born and a time to die,*
> *a time to plant and a time to uproot,*
> *³a time to kill and a time to heal,*
> *a time to tear down and a time to build,*
> *⁴a time to weep and a time to laugh,*
> *a time to mourn and a time to dance,*
> *⁵a time to scatter stones and a time to gather them,*

> *a time to embrace and a time to refrain from embracing,*
> ⁶*a time to search and a time to give up,*
> *a time to keep and a time to throw away,*
> ⁷*a time to tear and a time to mend,*
> *a time to be silent and a time to speak,*
> ⁸*a time to love and a time to hate,*
> *a time for war and a time for peace. (3:1–8)*

The Poem: Creation's Order and Balance (3:1–8)

Try reading the poem slowly out loud, pausing after each line. It's a rather thought-provoking, atmospheric, and beautifully balanced observation.

Verse 1 states the basic point. Everything has its time, and there is a time for everything. The whole of our life is governed by the way different things "fit" into the time allotted for them. Things "fit" not only in the sense of fitting into some time or other but also being the "*right* fit" for this time or that. Some things will be fitting here and now that will not be fitting at some other time or place.

The list of pairs is interesting.

- Sometimes the opposites are positive and negative (vv. 2, 3).
- Sometimes the opposites have to do with our working lives (vv. 2b, 3b, 5a, which probably refers to agriculture and building).
- Sometimes the opposites are strongly emotional (vv. 4, 5b, 8a).
- Sometimes the opposites operate within relationships (vv. 5b, 7b).
- Sometimes the opposites seem to be purely pragmatic (v. 6).

And so we could go on. The more we reflect on each line, the more the poem sends our minds into a whole variety of imaginary scenes and familiar experiences that we all recognize. It also ranges over a very wide spectrum of human life—personal, social, and even international.

But what is the poem "saying"? Well, of course, like much poetry, interpretation is in the mind of the reader. But at least two layers of meaning seem implied—and there may well be others.

First, life has its inexorable rhythms and oscillations. This may give life a refreshing variety. Things change and swing from one thing to another. We don't get bored with the same thing "all the time." Life itself is "timed"—by the sun and moon, by day and night, by seasons and weather, by the rhythm of the weeks. On the other hand, the poem as it is read aloud could begin to sound like the same repetitive futility that we found in the poem about the circularity of life in 1:4–11. Time *seems* to keep changing, but perhaps it's just going round and round. Or just swinging back and forth like a pendulum. Time for this; time for that. Tick tock; tick tock. Maybe. But perhaps something deeper comes to mind.

Second, time is always "for" something. Time is not neutral. It is not "mere time," an abstract function of our space-time universe. Time is more than the impersonal consequence of the expansion of the universe and the spinning of the earth on its axis and its planetary orbiting of the sun. Time is always full of content. Time is "for" things. Time challenges us with the question, "What time is it?" And that question usually means more than "Please look at the clock and tell me the time." It implies, what should we be *doing* right now?

And then, time challenges us regarding the right response to whatever time it happens to be for us now. Time's challenge might be, "GO FOR IT; don't miss this opportunity!" But on the other hand, time's challenge might be, "WAIT; it's not the right time for that just now."

That's also why we talk about "seasons of life." Some things are appropriate at a certain age but not at another. Now, at my age, would not be a good time for me to take up rugby again. But when I was fifteen and fit enough to play rugby, it would not have been the right time to put me in charge of a global mission organization like the Langham Partnership.

Now, in the book of Proverbs, part of the wisdom of the wise lies in exactly this—knowing what is fitting and appropriate in any given circumstances or time. The assumption is that *God* has ordered his creation in this way. There is a system and order to life; time is not just random or empty. It is part of God's creation. Time is part of the way God has given structure to our lives—personally and socially. Time is one of the blessings and gifts of creation to us—ever since the separation of night and day in Genesis 1. So *wisdom lies in understanding what fits any given time.* We need to respond rightly and choose wisely, in accordance with how things work. "Get with the program!" Wise living means living in tune with God's created order—including created time.

So at least part of the implied message of the poem is this: wisdom means knowing what time it is. And knowing how to act, or how not to act, in the light of that understanding.

However, after the poem comes the pondering.

The Pondering: Hints of Eternity and Limits of Time (3:9–15)
a) The Key Question Again (3:9)

As soon as he finishes his poem, Qoheleth comes back to his key question, the one he asked when he was launching his whole quest in 1:3.

> *What do workers gain from their toil? (3:9)*

It's as if he says to us. "Nice poem, don't you agree? I hope you understand something of what it means. But what good does it do you, living and working in this time-structured world?"

Or think of it like this. If all those balancing times are somehow "God's times," corresponding in mysterious ways to the rhythm and structures of time that God has built into creation, then what is the value of human labor in "our times"? Just knowing there's a right time for everything doesn't really answer the fundamental question. Even if you get your timing right, what's the point of it all?

That's a question that Qoheleth is finding so hard to answer. In fact, it's a hard burden God has put on us all.

I have seen the burden God has laid on the human race. (3:10)

Then Qoheleth answers his burdensome question in two ways: on the one hand (in verse 11), he answers it from what he can see coupled with what he cannot see but suspects must be true; and on the other hand (in verses 12–15), he answers it from what he knows on the basis of his strong Israelite faith.

b) First Answer: From What He Can and Cannot See (3:11)

Verse 11 is one of several key verses in the book. It expresses both a profound truth and a profound enigma.

He [God] has made everything beautiful in its time. He has also set eternity in the human heart; yet no one can fathom what God has done from beginning to end. (3:11)

Qoheleth acknowledges that "time," as he has observed it, is *God's* creation. Time is part of God's good and beautiful creation. There is a time for everything, so that everything is "fitting," beautiful, in its proper time. Time is like a great, big, beautiful tapestry telling a wonderful story, spread across yards and yards of the wall of some great mansion. Everything in the tapestry of time is beautiful in its own place in the overall picture and the unfolding story.

And because we can see part of that beauty, in whatever part of the tapestry of time we ourselves happen to live, we intuitively suspect that there must be a whole tapestry. Indeed, we suspect there must be something even beyond the tapestry—a wall stretching out on either side or a whole room in front or behind the tapestry.

The bit of the picture we can see is wonderful in itself, but it points to something even bigger and greater, some real-life reality that the tapestry is part of, something that contains the tapestry but is not contained within it.

We know that some bigger reality must exist than just the small part of the tapestry of time we can see because we live there. In fact, we suspect that there must be a whole tapestry far wider than our small part, but we can't see or grasp the meaning of the whole tapestry from one end to the other.

Why not? Because we live within the tapestry!

Qoheleth makes that into a condensed theological statement in three parts in verse 11:

- God has made the wonders and beauty of time. We can observe that by our experience of living in God's creation, of which time is an integral part.
- God has put eternity in human hearts. We sense that in our hearts; it is an intuition that God has put into us as creatures made in God's image who know our Creator.
- But we can't fathom what God has done from beginning to end. Our knowledge is finite and bounded. We cannot see much before or beyond our own time, let alone the whole of historical time, past or future.

Our minds can understand that there is a pattern to the times of life and history. So far so good. But we cannot see far enough in either direction to know the origin or the end point, let alone the purpose of the whole. Like a character woven into the tapestry itself, we may just be able to poke our heads out an inch or two, look around us a bit and see the immediate past and future of our own part of the story. But we can't step right out of the tapestry far enough into the room to see the whole thing. We don't have the elevation or perspective (from within the tapestry) to see and understand the whole tapestry of time, its origins and its ultimate purpose and goal.

Interestingly, science is probing further and deeper in the first direction, that is, back to the *origins* of time and space. With incredible tools and instruments, they are able to "see" to within micro-seconds of the Big Bang. But they cannot observe that event itself, the singularity when all the forces in the universe were concentrated in an infinitesimally small density. So yes, we can explore backwards in time (almost) to the origin of the universe. But science (in its contemporary form) refuses to ask, let alone try to answer, the question in the opposite direction—*what is it all for?* Is there some design, or purpose, or end goal for this inexorable flow of creational time? "Where will it all end?" is the popular despairing question about the problems of life. But the more important question is, "*For what end* did it all begin?"

And that is a question that can be answered, not from within the limits of time and space itself but *only* by revelation from outside the tapestry by the one who created it in the first place and is weaving the threads together.

The meaning of the tapestry as a whole comes from its designer, not from the characters in the tapestry itself. They participate in the story he is directing to the conclusion he intends.

So you see, this is the roadblock that Qoheleth will come up against again and again. He isn't going to get an answer to the meaning of life in this world from within the world itself by what his eyes can see. Mind you, he will keep on trying! But deep in his heart, he knows the limiting truth of what he has just said in verse 11 and will amplify it in verse 14. And that leads to his second answer.

c) Second Answer: From What He Knows (3:12–15)

There are two things Qoheleth says that he *knows* in these verses. Let's jump to the second in verse 14 for a moment and come back to verses 12–13 later.

As an Israelite, Qoheleth knows that God is the Creator and therefore God alone holds the key to understanding the whole tapestry. God can see the whole picture. God alone grasps the totality of life, the universe, and everything.

> *I know that everything God does will endure forever; nothing can be added to it and nothing taken from it. God does it* **so that people will fear him**. *(3:14; my emphasis)*

God is sovereign over time, and all his actions within history are enduring in their purpose and effects. Things may change with time (of course), but God's purposes endure forever.

So then, whether you read the poems of 1:4–11 (the cycles of life) and 3:2–8 (the rhythms of life) in a positive or negative way (or both), and as you apply them to your experience of life in all its variety, in the end God remains sovereign. And through all the changes and contingencies of time, God calls us to "fear" him (3:14b).

The fear of the Lord is a dominant theme in the wisdom literature (and Qoheleth will eventually get back to this just before he finishes). It is a repeated phrase in Proverbs,[1] and it was definitive of the character of Job.[2] It is a dominant theme in Deuteronomy.[3] It means not only that we should respect God's "Godness" and take him seriously; it also includes recognizing God's redeeming grace (in the exodus), trusting God's providence, obeying God's commands, and reflecting God's character. So this is one moment in the book when Qoheleth's Israelite faith sends a gleam of scriptural light through the darker clouds of baffled questions and skepticism.

And the next verse shines another beam of light. Here is something else that Qoheleth knows, not with the eyes in his head but with the eyes of faith.

---

1. E.g., Prov 1:7; 2:5; 3:7; 8:13; 9:10; 14:26; 15:16; 19:23; 23:17; 31:30.
2. Job 1:1, 8; 2:3; cf. 28:28.
3. e.g., Deut 5:29; 6:2; 10:12; 13:4; 14:23; 17:18–19.

> *Whatever is has already been,*
> *and what will be has been before;*
> *and God will call the past to account. (3:15)*

Now, the first two lines of verse 15 could be heard as a summary of that poem in chapter 1. It might look as if history is just one big repetition of the same old thing. But the last line injects a fundamental element of biblical faith. The God of biblical faith is the judge of all the earth who will do what is right. Ultimately God will call everything to account. There will be no loose ends. There will be nothing just swept under the carpet. The past lies open before God, and there will be a "putting right." This is, in fact, an important part of the biblical gospel. It is good news that evil and futility will not have the last word. God will do justice. God will come, as the end of Psalms 96 and 98 foresee, to judge the earth with righteousness and equity, and all creation rejoices at the prospect.

Also, if God was "there" in the past just as much as in the present, then nothing in the past, present, or future will get forgotten. Qoheleth amplifies this thought later in verse 17, which we'll come to in a moment.

Stepping back a little, we can come now to the first thing that Qoheleth says he knows, in verses 12–13.

> *12I know that there is nothing better for people than to be happy and to do good while they live. 13That each of them may eat and drink, and find satisfaction in all their toil—this is the gift of God. (3:12–13)*

Knowing that God is sovereign and just (vv. 14–15), we can accept wholeheartedly those aspects of life in God's creation that he gives us.

This is the second of his seven *carpe diem*, life-affirming passages. And it is the most straightforward of them all. He simply affirms the joys of life as God's gift, without any negative qualifications. Life *is good*, so enjoy it and *do good*. He uses the word "good" twice. And that of course recalls that strongly creational word from Genesis 1. Qoheleth is agreeing with God, who said seven times in Genesis 1 that what he had created is "good."

So it is, says Qoheleth. Enjoy it!

Once again, then, as we saw in 2:24–26, he has opened up a gap by putting contrasting statements side by side.

- We cannot fathom by observation the whole of the meaning of time and eternity; with our limited perspective there is so much that we simply do not know (though we can sense that there is an eternal reality beyond time itself; vv. 10–11).
- But we *do* know that God is in control and life is good (so enjoy life and do good; vv. 12–15).

This is a tension that we will find pulling in opposite directions all through the book, between the uncertainties of what we observe and the certainties of what we know by faith.

THE SCANDAL OF INJUSTICE (3:16–22; 4:1–3)

So, tracking with Qoheleth up to this point, we might be prepared to settle for just living with that tension. Maybe we could just accept it with some resignation or even a shrug: "Well, I know I'm never going to understand everything about this mysterious world and the way God has made it. But that's okay. I can live with that."

But just as we might be reaching that moderately comfortable thought, Qoheleth confronts us with one of the biggest scandals in human experience—the perversion of justice. Or, in the cry that come from every child's lips pretty early in life, "That's not fair!"

And I saw something else under the sun:

> *In the place of judgment—wickedness was there,*
> *in the place of justice—wickedness was there. (3:16)*

So brief, but so true. It's something we observe every day if we pay any attention to the news. "I saw . . . ," says Qoheleth. And so do we. Verse 16 puts into just twelve words of Hebrew one of the most appalling, frustrating, enraging, and disappointing facts of life in our world. Stuff happens that makes our blood boil and our anger spill out. Cheats, liars, con men, and crooks of every kind destroy other people's lives in multiple ways and are blatantly allowed to "get away with it."

It's not just that we know people behave badly. There are criminals and fraudsters out there. The real anger comes when we see that the very places where *justice should be done* have themselves become corrupted. That would include the organs of politics and government, the police, the courts, even businesses and financial institutions that should operate according to fair rules. But with Qoheleth we observe that even "there"—there *of all places*—we see wickedness, evil, injustice. It is just so utterly wrong. Deliberately perverted justice strikes at something very deep in our intuition of what it means to be human at all. Our anger is very real and justified—and is a pale reflection of God's response to the accumulation of what 3:16 describes.

A little later he comes back to this gloomy reality about human life with another astute observation.

> *[1]Again I looked and saw all the oppression that was taking place under the sun:*

> *I saw the tears of the oppressed—*
> *and they have no comforter;*
> *power was on the side of their oppressors—*

> *and they have no comforter.*
> *²And I declared that the dead,*
>   *who had already died,*
> *are happier than the living,*
>   *who are still alive.*
> *³But better than both*
>   *is the one who has never been born,*
> *who has not seen the evil*
>   *that is done under the sun. (4:1–3)*

These verses show that Qoheleth is no armchair cynic. He is not some professional observer, a hardened reporter on disaster scenes, an "objective" commentator with a camera crew, telling the story but keeping his own emotions at bay. No, he is deeply moved by what he sees. He feels genuine grief and pain at the oppression and suffering of the world.

And so does God. Oppression of the poor insults God: it hurts and grieves and angers him. Listen to some words in the book of Proverbs.

> Whoever oppresses the poor shows contempt for their Maker.
>   (Prov 14:31)

> Whoever mocks the poor shows contempt for their Maker.
>   (Prov 17:5)

> Do not exploit the poor because they are poor
>   and do not crush the needy in court,
> for the LORD will take up their case
>   and will exact life for life. (Prov 22:22–23)

The voices of the prophets are even more severe. Read Isaiah 58:6–10, or Ezekiel 22:6–12, or Amos 2:6–7. That's just a very small selection of texts that express God's reaction to systemic injustice and oppression of the poor and vulnerable.

And surely our own hearts resonate, however faintly, with God's attitude toward such oppression and suffering of the world's poor and marginalized. How can we cope emotionally with the sheer scale of suffering in our world? We see only a fraction of it. How does God cope with all of it? God sees and knows the suffering of every mother with her starving or injured child; every bereaved parent; every homeless, workless, stateless refugee; every trafficked and violated girl and woman; every enslaved child laborer; every tangled, poisoned, or stranded creature—every sparrow that falls to the earth (Matt 10:29–31)! It's not just a world that baffles our understanding; it's also a world we cannot bear to look at for long.

Coming back to Qoheleth, his pain is such that it leads him to the dreadful opinion he expresses in 4:2–3. It would be better to die and not have to see all the world's suffering anymore, he says. But it would be even better still never to have been born at all and so remain ignorant of the painful world of the living. This is the same grim sentiment that we find in the torment of Job 3:3–5 and Jeremiah 20:18.

But of course—what is "better" is not possible! It is not possible to be alive as a not-born person. This is the *terrible irony of human existence.* Existence is so painful that non-existence would be better! That is the kind of despair that some people sink into in our world still, with devastating consequences.

How can we respond to this horrible global reality—the pain and suffering of our world?

Once again, Qoheleth responds in two utterly opposite ways—leaving us to stagger in between them, scratching our heads and puzzling out what he really, really means!

In 3:17 he gives us his *confessional* response: what he believes.

In 3:18–20 he gives us his *observational* response: what he sees.

What He Believes (3:17)

I said to myself,

> "*God will bring into judgment*
> *both the righteous and the wicked,*
> *for there will be a time for every activity,*
> *a time to judge every deed.*" *(3:17)*

In verse 17 Qoheleth picks up again the theme of his poem about time. If there is a time for everything, and if God rules over time, then we can be sure that there will be a time for judgment. We are baffled and angered by injustice in the world. But *God* knows the difference between the righteous and the wicked and will deal with both appropriately. And God knows everything that is done within the whole of human history—past, present, and future. Therefore, God will be the final judge of all human conduct. And his judgment will be based on that total knowledge in a way that no human judgment can ever be.

In his negative moments, Qoheleth fears that all life on earth is merely circular and that everything will get forgotten in the great swirling vortex of universal time. But those fears are answered by the knowledge that God is sovereign over the whole of created time and all of it will be accountable to him. Past events are not "lost." Qoheleth does believe in the justice and the judgment of God. And he sees that as something positive to hold on to. This is a truth that Qoheleth glimpses rather fleetingly. But to grasp it fully we need the rest of the Bible's story, including its climax in Christ and completion in Revelation. Ecclesiastes 3:17 states a foundational element of the biblical faith and worldview: God is the final auditor and arbiter of all history and all human activity. Thank God!

For about ten years, I took up the enjoyable recreation of refereeing rugby matches (having been a player and still a great fan of the game). The referee is accorded great authority by the players.

They may not always agree with his decisions, and he doesn't always get them right. He can't see every infringement every time. Nevertheless, as the book of laws of the game states, "The referee is the sole arbiter of fact on the field." Whatever the ref decides—that's it! Nowadays, of course, the referee can refer decisions to another authority, the TMO, the Television Match Official, who can agree with or modify the referee's initial on-field decision. But eventually, even after consultation, the referee's decision is final.

God is the sole arbiter of fact on the field of all human activity, the final decisive authority, the ultimate judge of all people, all events, all claims. And God does not need a TMO! Nor does God need to watch replays from multiple angles! God sees and God knows. God knows the what and the why, the actions and the motives. That is the affirmation (breathtaking when you stop to think about it) of Psalm 33, which would have been part of the theological background to Qoheleth's own assumption in 3:17.

> [13]From heaven the LORD looks down
>   and sees all mankind;
> [14]from his dwelling place he watches
>   all who live on earth—
> [15]he who forms the hearts of all,
>   who considers everything they do. (Ps 33:13–15)

But knowing that God is the final judge is also a concealed hope. For, as Abraham could remind God himself, "Will not the Judge of all the earth do right?" (Gen 18:25). Old Testament Israelites knew that the righteousness by which God judges the wicked is the same righteousness by which God vindicates, saves, and redeems (e.g., Isa 45:21–25). *God will do what is right*, both in condemnation and in salvation. God will always be faithful to his covenant promises as well as his covenant threats. So the psalmists appeal to God's saving *righteousness* again and again.

They celebrate "the righteous acts of the Lord"—meaning those great acts of God's salvation like the exodus.

Qoheleth, as an Israelite who knew the Scriptures and the story they told, should have known and remembered something of those saving promises and actions of God, as a bulwark of hope in the midst of the horrors of injustice in the world. But while he acknowledges the reality of God and expresses this article of faith in God being the final judge, he pays little attention to that great redemptive story and sinks back instead into what he can see around him. And he finds no comfort there. Quite the opposite.

What He Sees (3:18–20)

What he sees is that people die in the same way as animals die. So, suppose you die *before* you see God's judgment on the wicked or his vindication of the righteous, that is, before you have a chance to witness verse 17 actually carried out? Suppose all you ever see from one end of life to the other is the scandalous wrongness of verse 16 and the sickening pain of 4:1–3? What then? Are you any better than the beasts?

> [18]*I also said to myself, "As for humans, God tests them so that they may see that they are like the animals.* [19]*Surely the fate of human beings is like that of the animals; the same fate awaits them both: As one dies, so dies the other. All have the same breath; humans have no advantage over animals. Everything is meaningless.* [20]*All go to the same place; all come from dust, and to dust all return."*
> *(3:18–20)*

Verses 19–20 are simple, indisputable facts of observation. They are also completely true at their own level. In purely material terms, there really is no difference between a human corpse and a dead cow or a dead dog. We share the same cocktail of biology and chemistry. We share the same "breath of life"—the created life that God gives to all living creatures (Gen 1:24, 30;

2:7; 6:17; 7:22). And as the psalmist says about all creatures, when God takes away their breath, "they die and return to the dust" (Ps 104:29). Death devours all of us, humans and beasts. And the brutal truth of Genesis 3:19 takes over—"Dust you are and to dust you will return."

Indeed, Qoheleth views this as something God wants us to remember (v. 18). We humans *know* that we are going to die! (Presumably the animals don't, though we've no way of telling.) The anticipated reality of death then becomes a kind of test. We need to be humble enough to know that we are creatures of the earth, dust, mortal. This is what God told us in Genesis 3, and only arrogant fools (or fictional superheroes[4]) think otherwise.

Qoheleth's point here is not quite the same as the one he made in chapter 2:14–16. Back then his complaint was that death makes the wise no better than the fool in the end. But here it's even worse. Death makes humans no better than animals. Man or beast, when you're dead, you're dead. What's so great about being a dead human instead of a dead animal? What's the point of even being human at all then? Nothing but *hebel*!

What Nobody Knows (3:21)

Ah but, you may object, that may be true of our bodies, but you're forgetting the spiritual difference. Surely when human beings die their spirit goes up (to God or somewhere), whereas animals' spirits simply go down into the earth.

The Hebrew words *ruah* and *neshamah* are very broad in meaning; they can mean spirit, breath, wind, life force. Qoheleth knows that God gives "spirit" to all living creatures, including human beings. If that were not so, we'd all perish—humans or animals. Qoheleth would have agreed with Elihu.

---

4. It is said that the great boxer Muhammad Ali, when asked by a flight attendant on a plane to fasten his seat belt, boasted, "Superman don't need no seat belt." To which the sharp young lady replied, "Superman don't need no plane."

> [14]If it were his [*God's*] intention
>> and he withdrew his spirit and breath (*ruah* and
>>> *neshamah*)
> [15]all humanity would perish together
>> and mankind would return to the dust. (Job 34:14–15)

The Bible teaches that both humans and animals have "spirit" in the sense of physical breath and animate life force. As we saw above, Genesis affirms this about all living creatures. They live because God gives them "the breath of life."[5] So neither Genesis nor Ecclesiastes is talking about a "soul," something that we humans have but animals don't. No, the same "spirit" from God that gives *us* life and breath is given to all creatures that live and breathe. We've got it and so have they because God gives it to both.

Now you may like to tell Qoheleth that our human spirit is somehow superior to an animal spirit, that our spirit goes "up" somewhere while their spirit just goes "down" to, well, the dust. And actually, a bit later Qoheleth will admit that he believes that too. For in his final poem, he talks about how at death, "the spirit returns to God who gave it" (12:7). And there were others in Old Testament Israel who had some hope that God would not allow his relationship with the godly simply to perish when they died, as for example the author of Job (19:25–27), or David (Ps 16:9–11), possibly Hannah (1 Sam 2:6), or the composer of Psalm 49, below. Somehow God would redeem their lives. It was all a bit of a mystery—a mystery to which the Israelites didn't bother to give much attention. They concentrated on the goodness (or problems) of life in this world and were content to trust God as Lord of life *and* death.

Psalm 49 shares some of the mood of Ecclesiastes but expresses a more positive hope in the end, even if he doesn't explain what he thinks it might mean.

---

5. Gen 1:30; 2:7; 6:17; 7:15, 22.

⁷No one can redeem the life of another
    or give to God a ransom for them—
⁸the ransom for a life is costly,
    no payment is ever enough—
⁹so that they should live on forever
    and not see decay.
¹⁰For all can see that the wise die,
    that the foolish and the senseless also perish,
    leaving their wealth to others.
¹¹Their tombs will remain their houses forever,
    their dwellings for endless generations,
    though they had named lands after themselves.

¹²People, despite their wealth, do not endure;
    they are like the beasts that perish.

¹³This is the fate of those who trust in themselves,
    and of their followers, who approve their sayings.
¹⁴They are like sheep and are destined to die;
    death will be their shepherd
    (but the upright will prevail over them in the morning).
Their forms will decay in the grave,
    far from their princely mansions.
¹⁵*But God will redeem me from the realm of the dead;*
    he will surely take me to himself.
        (Ps 49:7–15; my italics)

You see? We might say to Qoheleth, *That's* what we should believe. Of course, we *do* die just like the animals—we can all see that. But *our* spirits will "go up" and be safe in God's hands.

But, answers Qoheleth, how do you *know*? Have you ever seen that happen? Where's your empirical evidence that human beings somehow go on into a different, or better, or "up there" kind of life—whereas animals don't?

*Who knows if the human spirit rises upward and if the spirit of
the animal goes down into the earth? (3:21)*

He doesn't deny the possibility. He merely asks the question.
But it is a devastating question.

"Who knows?" I don't, says Qoheleth, and you don't either.
And maybe we can never know. So you'd better think hard about
the grounds on which you base your assumptions if you think you
do know. Justify your epistemology if you're going to make such
claims. "Who knows . . . ?"

Ecclesiastes 3:21, then, is another one of the "gap" places in the
book. Its sharp and challenging question opens up the tension and
apparent contradiction between the positive affirmations of verses
17 and 22 (which we'll come to in a moment) and the negative
observation of verses 18–20. We believe *that . . .* but we see *this.*
And by empirical observation alone, we can't get any further. We
simply cannot *know* if what we believe and hope is true or not. Not
by just looking, anyway. Observation alone cannot certify faith.

Even the structure of the text suggests this sense of a gaping
chasm. Verses 17 and 22 are on the outer edges of his reflection, sol-
idly hammered in place on either side. But in between them comes
the bleak void of death—human and animal death. And what's
the difference anyway? What can bridge the chasm?

Indeed, that kind of oscillation between some strong affirmations of faith and some depressingly negative observations of life as
we know it is a marked feature of this whole chapter. Perhaps this
is Qoheleth's way of expanding the oscillation of "times" in the
opening poem. He just swings from one thought to its apparent
opposite and back again. Watch the pendulum:

- Toil and burden (vv. 9–10)
    o God's beautiful creation and eternity in our hearts
      (v. 11a)
- But we can't fathom the whole story (v. 11b)

- ○ *Carpe diem*—life affirming (vv. 12–13)
- God is the sovereign and final judge (vv. 14–15)
  - ○ But injustice thrives down here (v. 16)
- But God will sort it out in the end (v. 17)
  - ○ Meanwhile, we all just die, no different from animals (vv. 18–21)
- *Carpe diem*—affirm life anyway! (v. 22)

So How Should We Then Live? (3:22)

So I saw that there is nothing better for a person than to enjoy their work, because that is their lot. For who can bring them to see what will happen after them? (3:22)

In this last verse of the chapter Qoheleth returns, for the third time now, to his more positive self. Even if Genesis 3 is the reality for us all, even if the dust of death awaits man and beast, Genesis 1 and 2 are still there. It is still a good thing to enjoy life and work in the present. That's our duty, our allotted function in life. At least in part, that is what we were created for—to work as creatures made in the image of God with authority and responsibility within creation. Get on with it and enjoy it!

Yet even as he sounds that positive, life-affirming note, he cannot resist a qualifying negative at the end of the verse. Yes, we should accept our creational role, responsibility, and the privilege of enjoying it, but one reason we should indeed get on with it right now is because we've no idea what's coming next! We cannot see or know the immediate future, let alone what awaits us after death.

Once again, then, we are left with the open question that is driving Qoheleth's quest. We are still walking alongside him on this journey of "faith seeking understanding"[6] (but not succeeding very much—yet).

---

6. From the Latin phrase coined by Anselm of Canterbury (c. 1033–1109), *fides quaerens intellectum*, referring to the theological method of Augustine of Hippo (AD 354–430).

He wants to affirm the truth of verses 12–13 and 22a, and he does so, strongly and with conviction, and will repeat it four times more in the book. But he cannot get away from what the eyes in his head tell him. The truths of his faith seem to be contradicted by the facts of 3:16 and 4:1–3 (human wickedness and suffering) and the enigma of 3:18–20 (human death).

"I'm sure this is true," he says, "that life is God's good gift and we should gratefully enjoy all that it brings us by way of food and drink and work. Yes, I believe that. But I just can't see how that can possibly square with the horrible facts of life and death in this crazy world. It is all *hebel* to me, an utterly baffling enigma. Maybe it's not merely baffling but actually pointless, completely meaningless, after all. I haven't found any satisfying answer yet. But let's keep trying. . . ."

I wonder if that describes something of the journey of many Christian believers? We talk sometimes about trying to achieve a "work-life balance." But we also struggle with a "faith-life" balance. We live with the tension between what we know and believe on the basis of faith in God and God's revelation in the Bible and what we see around us in the lives of others and ourselves. Faith and life sometimes seem to pull in diametrically opposite directions. And being the rope in the middle of that tug-of-war can be very uncomfortably stressful at times.

Is there any way we can respond, at least for the moment—today—before we journey on with him? Well, perhaps we can do two things with him, which lead to a third.

First, we can choose to know what he knows. We can affirm with him, and with greater certainty in the light of the rest of the Bible, the things he touches on in this chapter. These include:

- There is eternity beyond time, even if we cannot fathom time itself, let alone eternity (e.g., Ps 90:2).
- God is sovereign and is the ultimate auditor of all that happens "under the sun" in human history (e.g., Ps 33:10–15).

- There will be a final judgment, which will take all things into account and will be utterly just and rectifying. God will do what is right and put all things right before making all things new (e.g., Gen 18:25; Rev 20–22).
- Life is God's good gift in God's good creation and is to be affirmed and enjoyed (e.g., 1 Tim 4:4).

Let's join Qoheleth in those robust affirmations.

Second, we can choose to see what he sees—and feel what he feels. I say "choose to" since it is very easy for us not to—especially those of us living in relatively secure and comfortable circumstances. We can sense that there is not just frustration and bafflement in Qoheleth's observations of the wickedness and suffering of the world, but also a heart filled with grief and anger. What he sees is not merely topsy-turvy; it is also just plain wrong, intolerably so. And to the extent Qoheleth faintly echoes the heart of God on these evil facts of human life, we can and should amplify the echo in our own hearts. Let us not be complacent about the evils and suffering that we see in the world but be genuinely grieved and angry about them—as God is.

But surely and thirdly, we can go further. We can pray like the psalmists—who protest and plead in the presence of God, for him to do something about the wickedness and injustice they saw around them. So much Christian prayer seems bland and insipid compared to the language of, say, Psalm 10 or 94 and others. When do we ever have the boldness to pray like that in our churches? We can hear the prophets, too, and add our voices to theirs in standing against injustice and oppression and advocating on behalf of the poor and exploited. We can hear Jesus, too, and work out what it could mean in practice for us to trust our heavenly Father and then to "seek first his reign and his justice" (Matt 6:33; my own translation). And of course, we can and should *act* on what we know, see, feel, and hear in the Scriptures. As we shall see later, the New Testament gives us compelling reasons, beyond what

Qoheleth could have known, to be "doers of good" in the world of everyday life and work.

In other words, even while we accompany Qoheleth on his journey and must walk alongside him with integrity, listening with full attention to his struggles, we remember that we also live within the rest of the whole Bible's story. As we shall see, there is more to be *known* than he could see. And there is more to be *done* on the basis of what we know, even in the midst of life's baffling contradictions.

QUESTIONS FOR REFLECTION AND DISCUSSION

1. Do you find the rhythms of life (times and seasons, 3:1–8) reassuring, or just boring—or what? Why so?
2. In what ways do you find among non-Christian friends and colleagues that "God has put eternity in their hearts"? And how can we respond to that?
3. Why were injustice and oppression so troubling to Qoheleth (3:16–4:3)? Should they be more troubling to us than they usually are? And, in the face of global injustice, can we overcome the tension between the faith conviction of 3:17 and the pessimistic uncertainty of 3:19–21?

AMBIGUITIES OF WORK, POLITICS, WORSHIP, AND WEALTH

Ecclesiastes 4:4–6:12

So far in Qoheleth's quest for answers to his questions about the purpose or profit of life in God's puzzling world, he has taken us on a guided tour of his own experiments to try to find the meaning and point of life in chapters 1–2. Then in chapter 3 he paused for a more reflective moment, pondering the oscillating pendulum of time and the matching apparent opposites of what faith affirms and what observation sees (or cannot see).

Now he moves on and invites us to take a look at the lives of others in different areas of public life: workers, politicians, worshipers, and wealthy business people. His observations are sharp and often uncomfortable, sometimes positive, sometimes devastatingly honest. Through short proverbial verses or longer vignettes, he exposes truths that we can't ignore, gives us some good advice, and confronts us with sober warnings.

And in the midst of it all, he is still asking his key thematic question: "What do we gain from all of this work and activity?" What's the point of life? There must be some good to life, but who can tell what it is for sure? That's the provisional and pretty discouraging conclusion he comes to by the end this section, which is really the end of this first half of his book.

For who knows what is good for a person in life, during the few and meaningless days they pass through like a shadow? Who can tell them what will happen under the sun after they are gone? (6:12)

Who knows? Who can tell? It all ends with a shrug. Let's journey on to see how he gets to that depressing conclusion.

WORK: IT CAN BE SOUL DESTROYING (4:4–12)

Three times now Qoheleth has commended work as a good thing. Work is the gift of God to be enjoyed along with other gifts of creation, food and drink, and happiness. Work is a creational good.

Work is a Genesis 1 and 2 thing.

But frustration, enigma, folly, flaws, and sin have all permeated the world of work as well. Work is a toilsome burden in a fallen world.

Work is a Genesis 3 thing.

Qoheleth highlights in 4:4–12 two negative facts that are seen so much in the working environment. He is telling us yet again what he "saw" in his observation of life in his world. They sound just as familiar in our world as in his.

Competitiveness (4:4–6)

And I saw that all toil and all achievement spring from one person's envy of another. This too is meaningless, a chasing after the wind. (4:4)

"Envy" here is a strong word. It means jealousy and rivalry, the spirit of competitiveness taken to unhealthy extremes. And Qoheleth observes that this seems to be the driving force that makes people work so hard and so obsessively—even though he accepts that in the process a lot does get achieved.

There is a difference, of course, between this kind of unhealthy competitiveness (just being driven all the time by envy of others and wanting to get one over on them somehow) and a legitimate striving to do well, to excel, to succeed. There is nothing wrong with wanting to do the very best you can. The danger comes when that desire gets distorted into the desire to beat your neighbor in the process, trampling on him or her if necessary. And when that spirit becomes structured into whole economic systems, we end up with the cruel idolatry of naked capitalism, unfettered by any biblical moral principles. "Wealth is for the winners!" seems to be the slogan. The trouble is, however, as Craig Bartholomew puts it, "a society dominated by winners never knows what to do with the losers."[1]

But not only does unfettered, competitive envy produce losers as well as winners, with all the societal inequality that follows, it is also bad for your health. "Envy rots the bones," says Proverbs 14:30, an astute observation on the psychosomatic damage wrought by competitive stress. And in the end, it also becomes dehumanizing. The trouble with the rat race, as they say, is that even if you win the race, you're still a rat. As Jesus put it, "What does it profit a man to gain the whole world and forfeit his soul?" (Mark 8:36 ESV)—or their health or their marriage?

My son-in-law in his first job in a large accountancy firm was quite content for the moment with his position, his salary, and his working patterns and relationships. But then he was somewhat reprimanded by a colleague who told him he was not ruthlessly ambitious enough. "In this place," he was warned, "you're either on your way up or on your way out." What kind of working environment does that attitude produce? Nothing but *hebel*, says Qoheleth. You might as well chase after the wind.

So, if verse 4 is even a partially true observation, it's no wonder that Qoheleth asked that key question back in 1:3: "What do people gain from all their labors at which they toil under the sun?" Not a lot, even with competitive envy.

---

1. Bartholomew, *Ecclesiastes*, 196.

But then Qoheleth does it again! He just swings from one thing to its opposite in verse 5.

> *Fools fold their hands*
> *and ruin themselves. (4:5)*

If envy drives *over*work, then the remedy is not to give in to laziness. That's only for fools. The solution to work stress is not just to stop working and slack off! That will get you in just as much trouble in the end. Not much comfort then from Qoheleth, is there? Work is generated by envy. But laziness will ruin you.

Verse 6 switches gears yet again.

> *Better one handful with tranquility*
> *than two handfuls with toil*
> *and chasing after the wind. (4:6)*

Work hard, then, but make sure you take some rest. It is better to have even a small oasis (one handful) of peace of mind and tranquility than have both hands full of toil. Perhaps he is thinking of his creation theology again. God built rest into God's own "working week," as it were, and so should we.

But even then, after rest, when you throw yourself back into your work (v. 6b), it will turn out to be just "chasing after wind" anyway! Qoheleth knows how to spoil a good thing. Or rather, he knows that we have spoiled even good things that God gave us, like work and rest. The good thing of Genesis 1–2 has become the broken thing of Genesis 3. That's the reality of the world of work.

So, work is enigmatic. It is good, but it can be frenetically competitive. You need to rest, but you can't be lazy. And it can be as frustrating as herding cats.

Loneliness (4:7–12)

Next, Qoheleth observes another kind of worker—workaholics who end up utterly lonely because they are so absorbed and obsessed in their work that they never even pause to ask some pretty important questions.

> *⁷Again I saw something meaningless under the sun:*
>
> *⁸There was a man all alone;*
> * he had neither son nor brother.*
> *There was no end to his toil,*
> * yet his eyes were not content with his wealth.*
> *"For whom am I toiling," he asked,*
> * "and why am I depriving myself of enjoyment?"*
> *This too is meaningless—*
> * a miserable business! (4:7–8)*

Such a life is indeed meaningless and miserable. Of course, the person himself or herself can look very busy and very successful. They may be admired for their dedication and hard work, even held up as a role model for the young. Look how rich you can get when you put in the hours!

But if there is never any contentment with all the wealth that is gained by relentlessly obsessive work, what good is it? All that is left is just this driving compulsion to keep making more money. And the cost can be increasing isolation from all the relationships that make life worthwhile. You can end up as a very rich, very lonely, and very sad tycoon.

You might think that achieving wealth by hard work would produce the satisfaction of finding the meaning and purpose in life. But it doesn't, not by itself. The questions remain, as Qoheleth himself discovered in chapters 1 and 2.

The temptation to slide into the lonely misery of the workaholic is an easy one to fall into—especially for those of us with a robust work ethic and a sensitive conscience about laziness or procrastination. And perhaps most of all for those in some kind of church-paid Christian ministry. I speak from some experience. In my first few years as an ordained assistant pastor in a large church, I threw myself wholeheartedly, gladly, and conscientiously into "the Lord's work." It easily consumed all hours of the day (and sometimes the night), most days of the week. Not that I was in it for making money (far from it!), but for the Lord (of course). I got increasingly stressed out and curiously lonely and self-pitying under the pressures, until I received a good "talking-to" by my wife and another ordained colleague, who conspired to make me listen to them. I explicitly repented of the sin of thinking I was defined by my work output. I acknowledged the danger of workaholism and have sought to resist it ever since, though it is a recurring temptation.

Here's how it happens. Most of us, if asked what our fundamental loyalties and priorities are, would come up with something like: God first, then my spouse and family, then other people, then my work. In that order. But what happens when you are in church-paid Christian ministry? Ah, then you think of your work as "God's work." And, very subtly, that creeps up the priority level to where God himself alone should be. If your work is "for God," then, you presume, it must take top priority (because God does)—and everything else, including your spouse and family, slips down the ranking. And so one ends up in a kind of holy, spiritualized workaholism. Even "working for God" can become obsessive, driven, and relentless. And the very work you once loved can become a rest-less, lonesome, tyrannical burden. Or as Qoheleth puts it, "meaningless—a miserable business." How ironic and sad that even so-called God's work can end up feeling like that.

In verses 9–12, by contrast, Qoheleth points out the value of cooperation and community. He jots down a few, probably well-known, proverbs to make the point. And we'd all agree, in our heads at least.

⁹Two are better than one,
    because they have a good return for their labor:
¹⁰If either of them falls down,
    one can help the other up.
But pity anyone who falls
    and has no one to help them up.
¹¹Also, if two lie down together, they will keep warm.
    But how can one keep warm alone?
¹²Though one may be overpowered,
    two can defend themselves.
A cord of three strands is not quickly broken. (4:9–12)

Some of my African friends could add one of their familiar proverbs to his list: *"If you want to go fast, go alone. But if you want to go far, go together."*

And so, by putting his observation (v. 8) alongside his proverbs (vv. 9–12), Qoheleth has yet again created that puzzling gap that we are getting used to by now. For if working together is so good, and if there is so much strength and benefit in community projects and mutual support, then why are so many people desperately lonely—even in a busy workplace?

So then, although work is a good thing (Qoheleth will say it again and again), it is a very ambiguous good in this fallen world. By itself it can be soul-destroying in competitive and obsessive behaviors, and in the end it doesn't and can't provide the ultimate meaning for our lives. Indeed, when we think that it can, we turn work into an idol. A good thing becomes a god-thing, a false god. That way lies disaster.

POLITICS: IT CAN BE TRANSIENT (4:13–16; 5:8–9)

Qoheleth turns his gaze on the public world of politics and civil administration. And he sees all kinds of contradictions and enigmas there too.

Fickle Heroism (4:13–16)

[13]Better a poor but wise youth than an old but foolish king who no longer knows how to heed a warning. [14]The youth may have come from prison to the kingship, or he may have been born in poverty within his kingdom. [15]I saw that all who lived and walked under the sun followed the youth, the king's successor. [16]There was no end to all the people who were before them. But those who came later were not pleased with the successor. This too is meaningless, a chasing after the wind. (4:13–16)

This short tale may well be based on some actual events he witnessed. Or it may be that, by telling it in this nonspecific and anonymous way, Qoheleth gives us freedom to think of several possible examples of something similar, such as Pharaoh and Joseph, or Saul and David. At any rate, he sees some broader moral relevance in the sequence he portrays. An old and failing tyrant—who has stopped listening to anybody else; doesn't that sound familiar among political leaders?—gets replaced by a young, energetic, and wise new ruler. He had come from a very unpromising background but rises to the top and becomes everybody's hero.

But then what happens? It all goes horribly wrong, and the new ruler ends up just as unpopular as the one he replaced. It's a familiar sequence, even in modern democratic states. Some presidents or prime ministers get elected in a haze of messianic adulation and expectation. But the honeymoon period is short. Popular public heroes do not often grow old and stay heroes. Political popularity can be a very fickle thing. You might as well go chasing after the wind.

Qoheleth is commenting, then, on how received wisdom is easily subverted by events. "It's better to be wise even if you're young and poor than to be a rich old fool." Well, yes, we might all agree. That makes sense in theory. But even the new, young, wise ruler is likely to end up as unpopular and possibly quite as obstinate as his predecessor.

Bureaucratic Layers (5:8–9)

At the beginning of chapter 4, Qoheleth laments over the reality of social oppression and injustice. We can sense his grief as he witnessed the tears of the oppressed (4:1–3). But while it is certainly shocking to observe, he says, "Don't be surprised!" It's what happens when everybody is looking over their shoulder and passing the buck or the blame.

> *If you see the poor oppressed in a district, and justice and rights denied, do not be surprised at such things; for one official is eyed by a higher one, and over them both are others higher still. (5:8)*

The phenomenon he observes works at various levels to increase oppression. First of all, when there are layers of people responsible for any civic administration, it becomes so much harder for ordinary people to get access to anyone who can address their problem or grievance. Often people just give up in frustration and exhaustion—which is probably what the bureaucratic layers are hoping to encourage.

But second, when anything does go seriously wrong and there is some real injustice or scandal, the more layers of accountability there are, the easier it is to shift the blame in complicated circles and spirals without ever reaching a point where genuine blame and guilt can be assigned and brought to account.

On June 14, 2017, fire broke out in one apartment of a twenty-four-story apartment block in west London, UK, a block known as Grenfell Tower. The nature of the plastic cladding that had been affixed to the outside of the building enabled the fire to race upwards and around the building, engulfing the whole tower in an inferno in minutes. Seventy-two people lost their lives. It has become clear that the cladding was known to be unsafe but was a cheaper option than more fire-resistant materials.

So who was to blame? At the time of writing, an inquiry has been going on for years after the tragedy, but responsibility has been passed back and forth between the construction company, the manufacturers of the cladding, the local council who owns this unit of "social housing," the management company, and the building and fire-safety inspectors, all pointing the accusing finger anywhere else but themselves. Meanwhile the surviving residents and their families await any substantial kind of appropriate compensation, justice, or remedial action, while residents of other tower blocks with similar cladding find themselves living in fear of the same thing happening to them, having to pay exorbitant costs for the removal of the cladding, and unable to sell their homes and move elsewhere in the meantime. The labyrinthine tangle of outsourced contracts and management, of officials and executives, along with the possibility of corruption and profiteering, not only hampers the provision of decent and safe housing for the poor. It shows that excessive layers of bureaucracy such as Qoheleth so succinctly observed in his day are not only wasteful, but actually dangerous.

Verse 9 is very short and quite difficult to translate (even Qoheleth's Hebrew can be enigmatic!). Here are some different attempts:

> *The increase from the land is taken by all; the king himself profits from the fields. (NIV)*

> *But this is gain for a land in every way: a king committed to cultivated fields. (ESV)*

> *But all things considered, this is an advantage for a land: a king for a plowed field. (NRSV)*

> *Even the king milks the land for his own profit! (NLT)*

Personally, I can't be certain, but I think, in the context, that the NIV and NLT capture the intended flavor. The land is supposed to provide for everybody, but the king makes the biggest profit from it (perhaps referring to taxation or confiscation of land, such as Samuel warned the Israelites about, 1 Sam 8:10–18). If that is its meaning, then Qoheleth is challenging the trickle-down economic ideology of wealth, namely that if the rich are enabled to get richer, the benefits will trickle down to the poor. Nonsense, says Qoheleth. Wealth and power behave more like what we now know as capillary rise—they soak and suck upwards for the benefit of those at the top.

This author has perceptions and insights that are all around us still. He wrote in an ancient agricultural context, but he perceives processes at work in politics and economics that didn't die out with antiquity.

WORSHIP: IT CAN BE DANGEROUS (5:1–7)

Qoheleth is not altogether negative in what he has to say. Here for a moment he turns from observation to instruction and advice, sounding a bit more like the traditional wisdom of Proverbs. These verses are the most positive in the book until we reach the final chapter. What's more, these verses also make it clear that he is not an atheist or a skeptic. He understands how important it is to worship God with seriousness and sincerity. And as we'll see, he knows the Scriptures.

Listen More Than You Speak! (5:1–3)

¹Guard your steps when you go to the house of God. Go near to listen rather than to offer the sacrifice of fools, who do not know that they do wrong.

> *²Do not be quick with your mouth,*
> *do not be hasty in your heart*
> *to utter anything before God.*
> *God is in heaven*
> *and you are on earth,*

> *so let your words be few.*
> ³*A dream comes when there are many cares,*
> *and many words mark the speech of a fool. (5:1–3)*

"Watch your step!" The English idiom is exactly the same as the Hebrew and means the same: Be careful! The wisdom literature frequently uses the language of feet, steps, and walking along a path as metaphors for behavior (e.g., Prov. 4:10–19, and cf. Ps 1:1 and Ps 119 frequently). Just as we talk about "taking steps" to mean taking action, so in Hebrew they spoke of a person's steps to mean their habitual behavior.

So Qoheleth's warning means that just going to the place of worship (just walking in the gate of the temple courts or the door of a church) is not enough in itself. It is no substitute for living in accordance with God's ways. If you are going to plant your literal feet in the place where God is worshiped, you'd better make sure that your metaphorical feet have been walking in the ways that God has commanded.

Jeremiah gave a very severe warning about this to the people of Jerusalem, right at the gate of the temple courts. You can read the story in Jeremiah 7. Perhaps Qoheleth has this Scripture in mind in the warning he gives.[2] The people thought that so long as they kept coming to the temple and repeating all the right words again and again, they were safe. Not so, says God. You need to change your ways, or I will get rid of you from this very place.

> ³This is what the LORD Almighty, the God of Israel, says: Reform your ways and your actions, and I will let you live in this place. ⁴Do not trust in deceptive words and say, "This is the temple of the LORD, the temple of the LORD, the temple of the LORD!" ⁵If you really change your ways and

---

2. If so, it would mean that Ecclesiastes must be dated later than Jeremiah in the seventh century at least—as most scholars would reckon. But as explained in the introduction, the dating of the book is not at all agreed upon.

your actions and deal with each other justly, ⁶if you do not oppress the foreigner, the fatherless or the widow and do not shed innocent blood in this place, and if you do not follow other gods to your own harm, ⁷then I will let you live in this place, in the land I gave your ancestors for ever and ever. ⁸But look, you are trusting in deceptive words that are worthless.

⁹Will you steal and murder, commit adultery and perjury, burn incense to Baal and follow other gods you have not known, ¹⁰and then come and stand before me in this house, which bears my Name, and say, "We are safe"—safe to do all these detestable things? ¹¹Has this house, which bears my Name, become a den of robbers to you? But I have been watching! declares the LORD. (Jer 7:3–11)

Qoheleth would certainly have called the temple worship of the Jerusalemites "the sacrifice of fools," though if Jeremiah's accusation reflects their behavior during the rest of the week, it's hard to imagine that they didn't think they were doing anything wrong (v. 1). Samuel confronted Saul's sin and folly with a similar accusation. Saul had indeed offered a sacrifice, but it was in a state of impatient disobedience. So Samuel responded,

> Does the LORD delight in burnt offerings and sacrifices
> as much as in obeying the LORD?
> To obey is better than sacrifice,
> and to heed is better than the fat of rams. (1 Sam 15:22)

Qoheleth has good advice, then, for when we come to worship, especially for our Christian worship that is oh-so-wordy and talkative. Don't talk all the time! Don't fill every moment with your own words. Take time to listen. What God says to you is surely rather more important than what you have to say to God (though of course, God is indeed "all ears" to the praises, prayers, and protests of his people—as the book of Psalms show us clearly).

John Stott said that he owed his great love of the natural world, including especially his lifelong affection for birds, to his childhood walks in the countryside with his father, who would frequently scold him, "Shut your mouth and open your eyes!" Good advice, we may agree, except that "open your ears" would be more a more biblical instruction for our times of worship!

"God is in heaven and you are on earth." Even a simply stated truth like that shows us that Qoheleth is an orthodox believer. He shares the Old Testament Israelite understanding of God and humanity. And it challenges him (and us) to humility.

Be Careful What You Promise! (5:4–7)

⁴When you make a vow to God, do not delay to fulfill it. He has no pleasure in fools; fulfill your vow. ⁵It is better not to make a vow than to make one and not fulfill it. ⁶Do not let your mouth lead you into sin. And do not protest to the temple messenger, "My vow was a mistake." Why should God be angry at what you say and destroy the work of your hands? ⁷Much dreaming and many words are meaningless. Therefore fear God. (5:4–7)

Here is where we can see that Qoheleth knew his Scriptures. It's like he has just read these verses from Deuteronomy.

²¹If you make a vow to the LORD your God, do not be slow to pay it, for the LORD your God will certainly demand it of you and you will be guilty of sin. ²²But if you refrain from making a vow, you will not be guilty. ²³Whatever your lips utter you must be sure to do, because you made your vow freely to the LORD your God with your own mouth. (Deut 23:21–23)

And Qoheleth says, "Yes! Pay attention to that Scripture, and think carefully before you make a vow. Don't get caught out promising more than you can keep. God isn't fond of fools!"

And of course, he knows the words of wisdom that we find all over the place in the book of Proverbs: "The fear of the LORD is the beginning of wisdom." So he ends his advice for worshipers with this small gem of true biblical wisdom. It's short, but it's sensible. "Don't be a dreamer in your worship," he says, "Remember who it is you are worshiping. Fear God" (v. 7).

Considering the seriousness of Qoheleth's view of worship in these verses, then, it does seem that he has an anchor of faith in the midst of the tossing of his ship in the stormy sea of meaninglessness and all the enigmas of life. He *knows* that God is there and that God is to be worshiped with all due sincerity and truth. God is to be loved and feared, not treated lightly. This is a very important perspective for any believer to hold on to even when our experience of life in this world seems baffling and unfair.

Perhaps at this point on his quest, Qoheleth is going through something similar to the experience of the writer of Psalm 73. There we see a believer who struggles and puzzles over all the wrongness and unfairness of life in the world and the apparent futility of being a sincere worshiper of God at all. The psalmist wrestles with the same questions and absurdities as Qoheleth does. But then he moves from being deeply troubled and feeling he simply can't understand (v. 16) into the place of worship in God's sanctuary (v. 17). And it is there that things begin to look very different to him as a worshiping believer. Ultimate truths and ultimate destinies change his perspective on the present. Faith and trust in God's sovereign providence and goodness is restored.

Well, Qoheleth doesn't reach such a point of clear focus as Psalm 73 just yet. And we might wonder if he ever quite manages the clarity of the psalmist's faith. But at least he has affirmed something positive right here in the middle of the book and will expand on it a little more constructively at the end. Worship is a vital antidote to the worst of our depressing thoughts and experiences in life. And Qoheleth clearly has a high and serious view of the challenges that are involved in truly worshiping the living God.

WEALTH: IT CAN BE UNRELIABLE (5:10–6:12)

Qoheleth now turns from *social* corruption of the economy (5:8–9) to the kind of *personal* disasters that economic forces and financial unpredictability can produce.

Once again, we can take note of how cleverly he constructs his point. It's quite typical of the way he just puts opposites together. But this time he puts two things on opposite sides of a central fulcrum. At the center there is something he has "observed to be good" (5:18), but on either side there are things that he sees as meaningless and "a grievous evil" (5:13, 16; 6:2).

Look what forms the fulcrum at the center. It's 5:18–20, the fourth time he has made this robust, life-is-good affirmation. And this time he includes wealth as a good gift from God in itself.

But then on either side of that, like a sickening seesaw, he puts two things that might seem to contradict the central truth. Wealth? You might lose it all (5:10–17), and you might not even live to enjoy it (6:1–12). Let's take them in the order of the text.

You May Lose It All (5:10–17)

He starts with three quick proverbs in verses 10–12 about wealth. These are proverbs that we'd all probably agree with. This is standard wisdom stuff.

> *Whoever loves money never has enough;*
> > *whoever loves wealth is never satisfied with*
> > > *their income.*
> > *This too is meaningless. (5:10)*

Somehow, money is inherently unsatisfying. Or rather, by its nature it seems to generate increasing dissatisfaction. Does anybody ever say, "I'm rich enough now," and then stop wanting more? When Qoheleth says "whoever *loves* wealth . . ." he is agreeing with what the apostle Paul would later say. Money in and of itself is not the real problem. It's the love of it that is "a root of all kinds of evil" (1 Tim 6:10), because such love can never be content with "enough."

> *As goods increase,*
> > *so do those who consume them.*
> *And what benefit are they to the owners*
> > *except to feast their eyes on them? (5:11)*

As your wealth increases, so do costs and consumption. You start getting more demands, more expenses. So you don't feel any better off, just more hassled with responsibilities and pitfalls. All you can take pleasure in is staring at your bank balance or all the stuff you've acquired. And what real good is that?

> *The sleep of a laborer is sweet,*
> > *whether they eat little or much,*
> *but as for the rich, their abundance*
> > *permits them no sleep. (5:12)*

Wealth can of course be a form of security, but for some it only increases anxiety and worries compared to a simple, uncomplicated working life. The more you have, the more you worry. And that produces sleepless nights, perhaps (in view of the second line of the proverb) caused by indigestion after overeating! Ezekiel gives us a rather more caustic view of callous greed and gluttony: "Now this was the sin of your sister Sodom: she and her daughters were arrogant, overfed and unconcerned; they did not help the poor and needy" (Ezek 16:49—a text that might lie behind Jesus's parable in Luke 16:19–31).

And then, after his three proverbs, Qoheleth paints a tragic picture of loss and draws a bleak conclusion. His picture is familiar. We all know this kind of situation, perhaps in painful personal experience or just by watching the news.

> ¹³*I have seen a grievous evil under the sun:*
>
>> *wealth hoarded to the harm of its owners,*
>>> ¹⁴*or wealth lost through some misfortune,*
>> *so that when they have children*
>>> *there is nothing left for them to inherit.*
>> ¹⁵*Everyone comes naked from their mother's womb,*
>>> *and as everyone comes, so they depart.*
>> *They take nothing from their toil*
>>> *that they can carry in their hands.* (5:13–15)

So here is somebody who works really hard and makes a fortune. They've built up a really substantial investment, and they're all ready to hand it on as their legacy to their children. But CRASH! They lose it all. Qoheleth gives no explanation. It wasn't necessarily because of any wrongdoing or fraud. Maybe they made a disastrous deal that went belly-up. Maybe there were bad debts or a market collapse that wiped out their savings. Maybe there was a war or an invasion and they lost their land. Who knows? It doesn't really matter; the bottom line is that . . . there was no bottom line anymore. All gone. Nothing but the stark ending: he dies as naked as he was born. Like the rest of us.

John Stott, when he spoke about the dangers of being too attached to this world's goods, liked to tell the story of the lady who was attending the funeral of a man known to have been very wealthy. Curious about the size of his estate, she went up to the minister and whispered, "What did he leave?" To which the reply came, "Everything." John Stott would then conclude, echoing Qoheleth, "Since our lives are spent between two moments of nakedness, it is best to travel light."

That brings Qoheleth back to his key question—the one he asked at the start in 1:3. What do we gain from all our life's work?

> *16 This too is a grievous evil:*
>
> > *As everyone comes, so they depart,*
> > *and what do they gain,*
> > *since they toil for the wind?*
> > *17 All their days they eat in darkness,*
> > *with great frustration, affliction and anger. (5:16–17)*

If someone makes a lifetime of wealth but loses it and can't pass it on, what did they gain by all that? Nothing but wind, vapor, in the end. "It all went up in smoke," as we say. Too true. It all ends in lonely, miserable darkness.

But It Is Still the Gift of God! (5:18–20)

By now we might be used to this tactic, but it is still a shock. Qoheleth just swings from a bleakly negative "grievous evil" to a gloriously positive "good." Here is the fulcrum in the middle of the seesaw.

> *18 This is what I have observed to be good: that it is appropriate for a person to eat, to drink and to find satisfaction in their toilsome labor under the sun during the few days of life God has given them—for this is their lot. 19 Moreover, when God gives someone wealth and possessions, and the ability to enjoy them, to accept their lot and be happy in their toil—this is a gift of God. 20 They seldom reflect on the days of their life, because God keeps them occupied with gladness of heart. (5:18–20)*

At first sight, verse 18 might sound like an answer to the question of verse 16. What do you gain from a lifetime's toil? Well, this is what you gain—a life of enjoying the gifts of God, even if it seems like only "the few days of life." However, in the light of the case he's just presented, this is only a partial and not very satisfying answer in the context. For what if you don't get to enjoy those good gifts at all?

And did you notice one other sharp contrast? In verse 17 we see the poor, suffering tycoon, eating his food in lonely darkness, frustration, affliction, and anger. But in verse 18 we are encouraged to eat and drink with satisfaction, joy, and thankfulness to God. Really? How can we do that when we know there are so many in our world who live with food insecurity and constant hunger? And how can we cheerfully enjoy the other gifts of God that Qoheleth describes in verse 19 when we know of the millions who are unemployed and living in poverty or whose working lives are blighted by oppression and injustice, such as Qoheleth himself observes in 4:1 or 5:8–9?

But still, even aware of the baffling world out there, Qoheleth cannot shake off this settled conviction. There *is* a goodness to creation, and so God's gifts of life, health, food, work, wealth, and happiness are all to be received and enjoyed for what they are—God's gifts (he says that twice, so I can too!). I reckon the apostle Paul would agree (1 Tim 4:2–5). It's a God thing. It is noticeable that, whereas God is absent from the proverbs and observations of 5:8–17, God appears four times in these three verses (vv. 18–20).

And yet, however much he holds on to the truth and implications of Genesis 1 and 2, somehow Genesis 3 keeps butting back in. For God's ways are inscrutable. God may indeed grant you all of verse 19. But in this fallen world, what if he doesn't?

Verse 20 seems to answer with a shrug. It's best not to think about that too much. Life's too short. Just keep busy. Stay happy.

But is that an answer?

Not really.

For now we land on the other side of the seesaw.

You May Not Live to Enjoy It (6:1–12)

Qoheleth has described the person who gets very wealthy but then loses it all for some unknown reason (5:10–17). That was the other side of the seesaw. On this side now, he describes somebody who gets absolutely everything God could possibly give (it sounds like he has Solomon in mind again) but then ends up unable to enjoy it. They've got everything anybody could want—except the pleasure of enjoying it.

> *¹I have seen another evil under the sun, and it weighs heavily on mankind: ²God gives some people wealth, possessions and honor, so that they lack nothing their hearts desire, but God does not grant them the ability to enjoy them, and strangers enjoy them instead. This is meaningless, a grievous evil. (6:1–2)*

Once again, Qoheleth gives no reason. Perhaps it was ill health, a stroke, insanity, depressive illness, chronic and crippling pain—some condition in which you have to look on impotently as *other* people enjoy all *you* labored for, but you can't enjoy yourself. And if *you* can't enjoy it, what's the point of having gained it all in the first place?

Even if a man has a hundred heirs and lives twice a thousand years, if there is no *joy* in life for him, then his fate is worse than a stillborn baby. That's the most cruel and awful curse Qoheleth can think of.

> *³A man may have a hundred children and live many years; yet no matter how long he lives, if he cannot enjoy his prosperity and does not receive proper burial, I say that a stillborn child is better off than he. ⁴It comes without meaning, it departs in darkness, and in darkness its name is shrouded. ⁵Though it never saw the sun or knew anything, it has more rest than does that man—⁶even if he lives a thousand years twice over but fails to enjoy his prosperity. Do not all go to the same place? (6:3–6)*

Perhaps Qoheleth knew the book of Job and recalls that agonizing first heart-cry from Job in which he wishes he'd never been born at all or, failing that, had been born dead. Read the whole of Job 3 to feel the force of that emotion, which Qoheleth echoes here.

> [11]Why did I not perish at birth,
> and die as I came from the womb?
> [12]Why were there knees to receive me
> and breasts that I might be nursed?
> [13]For now I would be lying down in peace;
> I would be asleep and at rest. . . .
> [16]Or why was I not hidden away in the ground like a
> stillborn child,
> like an infant who never saw the light of day?
> (Job 3:11–13, 16)

Indeed, Qoheleth concludes that the person who cannot enjoy life after gaining so much wealth is even worse off than a stillborn baby. For the stillborn has known nothing of life and its wonderful gifts and pleasures and so will never miss what it never knew.

And anyway (in the last line of v. 6, Qoheleth returns to his obsession with death), we are all going to end up in the same place as a stillborn baby, whether you live only a fleeting moment or twice as long as Methuselah. Qoheleth really does have the gift of discouragement with this ruthless, relentless honesty. *Memento mori!* Remember you will die. We all will.

Just thinking about that gloomy prospect seems to send Qoheleth into a downward spiral, as the remainder of chapter 6 just drags on to a miserable end.

> [7]*Everyone's toil is for their mouth,*
> *yet their appetite is never satisfied.*
> [8]*What advantage have the wise over fools?*

> *What do the poor gain*
>> *by knowing how to conduct themselves before others?*
>>> *(6:7–8)*

Even if you fight your way to the top by hard work, wisdom, and social etiquette, what good will that do if you join the rich and sophisticated set but end up totally unsatisfied like one of those two people on either end of that horrible seesaw?

> *Better what the eye sees*
>> *than the roving of the appetite.*
>> *This too is meaningless,*
>>> *a chasing after the wind. (6:9)*

The NIV translation of verse 9a sounds very like a common English proverb, "a bird in the hand is better than two in the bush." That is, what you actually have right now is better than what you just dream of having. And that is most likely what he means.

However, the Hebrew of verse 9a could be translated:

> *The seeing of the eyes [that is, being alive in the world]*
>> *is better than the passing of life [that is, being dead].*[3]

Qoheleth is doing it again, you see, if that is what his words imply. It would be a typical example of his ironic self-contradictions.

- He *thinks*: It would be better to be born dead than to have riches but no joy (v. 3).
- But he *knows*: It's actually better being alive than being dead (no matter what; v. 9a).

---

3. See Bartholomew, *Ecclesiastes*, 237–38.

It is all just so unbearably baffling, "meaningless, a chasing after the wind" (v. 9b).

Life is an enigma.

Of course, as human beings we have figured out a great deal about life in this world.

> *Whatever exists has already been named,*
> *and what humanity is has been known;*
> *no one can contend*
> *with someone who is stronger. (6:10)*

We know what it is to be human. And we know how to name and classify and understand so much in creation; Qoheleth has read Genesis 2. Everything in creation stands under the sovereignty of God our creator, and he has given us responsibility and authority in creation. But in the end, we can't fully understand God himself, still less contend with him—God is probably the one meant by "someone who is stronger."

And talking about all this is not just wearisome. Actually, it seems that the more we talk about it, the worse our confusion will get!

> *The more the words,*
> *the less the meaning,*
> *and how does that profit anyone? (6:11)*

There it is again. Did you spot it? That last line of verse 11 is Qoheleth's *key question*, which he keeps coming back to again and again and again, ever since 1:3.

What's the profit? What's the point? Where does it all get us in the end? "How does that profit anyone?"

And this time he answers it with another *despairing* question: "Who knows?"!

For who knows what is good for a person in life, during the few
and meaningless days they pass through like a shadow? Who can tell
them what will happen under the sun after they are gone? (6:12)

Life *should* be "good" for people. That's how God created it to
be. That's what we believe. But who knows *what really is good for*
us? Who knows what is best? Who can show us the real meaning
of life? One lifetime seems far too short to find out. And beyond
that, we don't know what the future holds, or what lies after death
for us, or what will go on here on earth after we've left the party.

There are just too many unknowable unknowns, too many
unanswerable questions, too many inscrutables to unscrew, too
many things in this world that we don't understand.

So who knows what is good?

Well, Qoheleth is going to keep on trying to answer that
question with some more reflections in the next chapters. For the
moment, though, it's a pretty pessimistic place we've ended up.
But remember—*we're on a journey here*. And the journey is far
from over. The quest has a long way to go yet. This is only halfway
through the book!

As we pause with him at the end of this chapter, how do we
cope with the tensions he has stretched out for us—the tensions
between what he affirms about God and the goodness of life in
God's creation, on the one hand, and the depressing, frustrating,
and grievous realities he observes all around him, on the other hand?

Aren't his observations accurate? Don't we see and think the
same things?

Qoheleth has invited us to look at some big areas of life: the
world of work, the world of politics and economics, the practice of
worship, and the creation of wealth. And in each case we can see the
positive perspective of Genesis 1 and 2 and the disastrous impact
of Genesis 3. Work, society, worship, and wealth are all part of
God's good, created order. Yet at the same time every one of them

is corrupted and fractured and rendered potentially "meaningless" or baffling by sin and evil, the sheer absurdity of events, and the ultimate mystery of death.

We live in a world that we *are* capable of understanding to a large degree, since we can discover and explain so many of the good things God has given us in creation. And yet there remain dark mysteries and important questions that we can't satisfactorily answer. It's a world we both do and don't understand. And we cannot escape the challenge of living in the tension of that double reality.

QUESTIONS FOR REFLECTION AND DISCUSSION

1. What evidence or examples have you seen in the world of work of the kind of evils that Qoheleth observes in 4:4–8? How can we resist such dangers in our own working lives, whether in the world "out there" or in our so-called Christian work?

2. How do the warnings of 5:1–7 challenge our own church's practices of worship and our participation in them? What might "the sacrifice of fools" mean?

3. Would you agree with 5:10? How can we guard against the uncertainties and dangers of wealth that Qoheleth uncomfortably exposes—and yet still affirm 5:19?

THE DARKEST HOUR

Ecclesiastes 7:1–9:16

They say the darkest hour is just before the dawn. Personally, I've never tested that empirically, but it sounds plausible. Certainly, in this long quest on which we are journeying with Qoheleth, this section of the book (and especially chapter 9) reaches depths of dark despair that make the arrival of something positive and hope-filled in the final chapters a very welcome relief.

Nevertheless, there are some profound moments that will have us pondering deeply. In these three chapters we will encounter:

- a real theological insight that connects with scriptural teaching (at the end of chapter 7);
- a moment of great humility in a world of intellectual arrogance (at the end of chapter 8); and
- a wrestling with the awfulness of death that comes very close to destroying Qoheleth's faith in God and certainly does destroy his faith in his own ability to find what he's looking for by wisdom alone (in chapter 9).

So, although this may turn out to be the most depressing part of the journey, it will have its lighter moments, and let's be patient till we reach a slightly sunnier landscape in chapters 11 and 12, after something of a pause for breath in the interlude of proverbs in chapter 10.

WISDOM IS INSCRUTABLE (7:1–29)

Chapter 6 ended with a question: "Who knows what is good for a person in life . . . ?" Qoheleth seems to ponder that question in the first half of chapter 7. You'll see the word "better" in many of these verses. But actually, Hebrew did not have a word for "better." They just said, "This is good . . . *from* (meaning, in comparison with) that." So all those verses with "better" in them actually have the simple Hebrew word "good," as if answering that question in 6:12.

What Is Good for a Person? God Knows! (7:1–14)

"What is good?" "Well, maybe this is good, or maybe that is good, but I think you'll find this would be better," and so on. That's the way these verses work, but with a few surprises (and why is that not surprising?!).

Qoheleth runs through a number of common, though rather paradoxical, proverbs (in verses 1–6, 8–10), but then he mixes in and adds some of his own that seem to counteract and subvert the received proverbial wisdom (in verses 7, 11–12).

So he starts in 7:1 with a nice variation on Proverbs 22:1:

> A good name is more desirable than great riches;
>   to be esteemed is better than silver or gold.

Or, as Qoheleth turns it:

> *A good name is better than fine perfume. (7:1a)*

Your reputation matters more than your aftershave, chaps. Obviously! But then he goes on to reflect that what is *better* is not always what is *obvious*. And that is so especially if what you are seriously looking for are some clues to the meaning of life.

If, like Qoheleth himself, you are seeking some deep and

worthwhile reflection on what really counts in life (especially as we face the enigma of death), then in that search for ultimate meaning you will find that:

- Funerals are better than birthday parties

> *[1b]and the day of death better than the day of birth.*
> *[2]It is better to go to a house of mourning*
> *than to go to a house of feasting,*
> *for death is the destiny of everyone;*
> *the living should take this to heart. (7:1b–2)*

- Frustration may teach us more than laughter

> *Frustration is better than laughter,*
> *because a sad face is good for the heart. (7:3)*

> *Do not be quickly provoked in your spirit,*
> *for anger resides in the lap of fools. (7:9)*

- Better to be with those who mourn than with the "crackling" laughter of fools—the emptiness of so much that counts for entertainment.

> *[4]The heart of the wise is in the house of mourning,*
> *but the heart of fools is in the house of pleasure.*
> *[5]It is better to heed the rebuke of a wise person*
> *than to listen to the song of fools.*
> *[6]Like the crackling of thorns under the pot,*
> *so is the laughter of fools.*
> *This too is meaningless. (7:4–6)*

- Finishing something patiently is better than unfulfilled pride at the start.

> *The end of a matter is better than its beginning,*
> *and patience is better than pride. (7:8)*

- Nostalgia is pointless—very sound advice!

> *Do not say, "Why were the old days better than these?"*
> *For it is not wise to ask such questions. (7:10)*

If we idolize or romanticize the past, we forget its horrors also and the lessons Qoheleth has already made about how history seems to come round again and again.

This is all traditional wisdom, similar to the exhortations in Proverbs. These are the kind of things that a wise person would say. And that is Qoheleth's world; he himself is among the so-called wise ones! So he echoes what Proverbs says: you know where you'll find the wise man, so go along there and listen (v. 4). And you certainly need to listen to the wise, even if they rebuke you (v. 5). Qoheleth is commending his own profession and colleagues. *"Go and listen to the wise!"*

But then, with astonishing boldness, he subverts that advice by warning us that you can't always trust a wise person to do the right thing. At least, not if money is involved.

> *Extortion turns a wise person into a fool,*
> *and a bribe corrupts the heart. (7:7)*

The judgment of even the wisest judge or counselor can be distorted by extortion or bribery. Put enough pressure on somebody (e.g., threaten their children), and their wisdom turns to folly. Offer enough money to somebody, and you can destroy their "heart" (meaning their ability to make good decisions with integrity). Even wisdom is venal and corruptible, says wise man Qoheleth. Even wisdom can be "bought." That's a serious allegation, but we know it can be true in so many cases. As the criminal underworld boasts, with some justification, "Everyone has their price." And so-called objective and neutral science can be perverted by vested interests.

And while of course it's fine to be wise, it's even better if you have a good stash of inherited money too, just in case. . . .

> Wisdom, like [or probably, "with"] an inheritance, is a
>   good thing
> and benefits those who see the sun. (7:11)

Verse 12 sounds rather cynical—at least in its first half. Being wise is a good protection ("shelter") in life (we all agree). But then, so is having money!

> Wisdom is a shelter
> as money is a shelter. (7:12a)

Putting wisdom on roughly the same level as money does not sit comfortably with all those sayings in Proverbs that value wisdom higher than rubies, gold, silver, etc., and especially the one that prefers poverty lived in the fear of the Lord ("the beginning of wisdom") to "great wealth with turmoil" (Prov 15:16). Yet here Qoheleth virtually equates wisdom and money in their protective power—an astonishing subversion of core principles of Proverbs. And even the second half of verse 12 doesn't seem to help much. "*Wisdom preserves those who have it.*" Well, yes; but so does money, it seems, from 12a.

But that's just the way things are in this fallen, topsy-turvy world. Wisdom is great, but money talks. Proverbs sparkle in theory. But in real life stuff happens that seems all the wrong way round.

And here's the hardest thing: since *God* is in charge of life, the universe, and everything, that must be the way *God* has made it. Think about it:

Consider what God has done:

> *Who can straighten*
> *what he has made crooked? (7:13)*

If the world is bent—it's God's fault! God is the one who made it crooked. So you'll never be able to straighten it out or figure it out either. God's done it. Get over it.

Now I want to say immediately that this seems to me one of the places where Qoheleth says things we just can't agree with. And even Qoheleth himself doesn't agree with it later! He has a different perspective in 7:29, as we'll see. And yet, what he says is at least partially true in the light of Genesis 3. God pronounced a curse on the ground because of human sin and rebellion. And Paul interprets that in a way that would have had Qoheleth nodding in agreement: "For the creation was subjected to frustration, not by its own choice, but by the will of the one who subjected it" (*i.e., God*) (Rom 8:20). God did not *originally* make things all crooked and bent, but our sin has resulted in a world that God has subjected to all the futility, frustration, enigma, and meaninglessness that Qoheleth explores so ruthlessly.

But for the moment, at this point in his quest, all he can say is: enjoy the good days and make the most of the bad days. Every day comes from God, and you don't know what the future holds.

> *When times are good, be happy;*
> *but when times are bad, consider this:*
> *God has made the one*
> *as well as the other.*
> *Therefore, no one can discover*
> *anything about their future. (7:14)*

Now again, we could say that at one level, within a fully biblical understanding of God's loving providence in our lives, verse 14 can be a true and sensible way to live. Paul clearly expects bad times for believers but sees all our times as under God's sovereign governance. So yes, even if we cannot know our own personal future in this life at least (and that's all Qoheleth is thinking of right now), we can be assured that "in all things God works together with those who love him to bring about what is good" (Rom 8:28, NIV footnote alternative—which, I think, is the best translation), and nothing can separate us from the love of God.

But to be honest, Qoheleth isn't quite basking in Romans 8:28, is he? From the mouth of Qoheleth, verse 14 sounds not so much like an act of quiet trust as a shrug of exhausted frustration or even a touch of fatalism. Like the old Doris Day song (but without the cheerful music), "*Que será será*, whatever will be will be."

Stuff happens, for good or ill. You can thank God or blame God, whichever you prefer. It doesn't make much difference either way.

Life Is Unfair, So Hedge Your Bets (7:15–22)

Qoheleth turns from his musing on the crookedness and unpredictability of life to its unfairness. He is really upset by this, it seems, but doesn't have a very convincing response.

In this meaningless life of mine I have seen both of these:

> *the righteous perishing in their righteousness,*
> *and the wicked living long in their wickedness. (7:15)*

The technical term for this is the problem of theodicy—how can we justify the ways of God in the world. For if (as books like Deuteronomy and Proverbs say repeatedly[1]) God blesses the righteous and punishes the wicked, then why do some good people

---

1. See Deuteronomy 28–30 for an intense reinforcement of this aspect of the book's theology throughout, and read Proverbs 15 for a range of examples of God's reactions to the righteous and the wicked respectively.

die young and many bad people thrive into old age? "I've seen both of these!" says Qoheleth. It's an observable fact of life, and the writer of Psalm 73 would agree (as we've already seen).

So, since that's the case (and you can't say it isn't), then try to keep your head down and don't be too wise or too righteous—or too foolish or too wicked. Just cultivate a little bit of both.

> [16]*Do not be overrighteous,*
>   *neither be overwise—*
>   *why destroy yourself?*
> [17]*Do not be overwicked,*
>   *and do not be a fool—*
>   *why die before your time?*
> [18]*It is good to grasp the one*
>   *and not let go of the other.*
>   *Whoever fears God will avoid all extremes. (7:16–18)*

This is about as shocking as Qoheleth gets. For these verses seem to dissolve not only the distinction between wisdom and folly (a distinction that is utterly central to the whole wisdom worldview—just scan any chapter of Proverbs at random), but also the distinction between the righteous and the wicked (a distinction which is crucial to the whole covenantal worldview of Israel—and indeed the whole Bible).

I mean, look at verse 17: "Do not be overwicked." Can he be serious? You don't want to be *too* wicked—but (presumably) you can be *slightly* wicked if you need to be. A little wickedness is okay! It reminds me of a line in one of the songs in the musical *Matilda*, that when things aren't right,

sometimes you have to be a little bit naughty.[2]

---

2. From the song, "Naughty," by Tim Minchin, a song from the 2013 stage adaptation of Roald Dahl's book *Matilda* (London: Jonathan Cape, 1988).

That may sound fine and funny in a children's musical where kids do some pretty bad (but well-deserved and outlandish) things in order to deliver justice as they see it. But as a moral philosophy, it stands in a very different place from Leviticus 19:2, for example ("Be holy because I, the LORD your God, am holy"), not to mention all the teaching of Jesus.

The last line of verse 18 is puzzling. The NIV footnote may well be right. Qoheleth puts righteousness and wickedness side by side and suggests, not *"avoid all extremes"* but *"follow them both."* That is, have a foot in both camps. Feel at home among the righteous and the wicked. And once again we have to say, this dissolves a distinction utterly crucial to Proverbs, Psalms—and the whole Bible. And does Qoheleth really see such seemingly amoral advice as compatible with the fear of God? This is far distant from the stark binary choices that Proverbs set before those who fear the Lord, and, if that is what the verse implies, then the Frame-Narrator will correct it in 12:13.

Perhaps verse 19 is Qoheleth's way of pulling back from the stark implications of what he has just said (or may have said, if the possible interpretation of verse 18 above in the NIV footnote is correct), by emphasizing again the supreme value and priority of wisdom, by which he knows that the fear of the LORD would preclude such moral relativism.[3]

---

3. The NET Bible (2nd ed.) recognizes the possibility of the NIV footnote's translation but disfavours it for the very reason I have suggested above: could Qoheleth really have gone this far? Interpreting the words in that way might mean, "To adopt a balanced lifestyle that is moderately righteous while allowing for self-indulgence in moderate wickedness ("to follow both of them," that is, to follow both righteousness and wickedness). However, this seems to unnecessarily encourage an antinomian rationalization of sin and moral compromise." Instead, the NET Bible offers the translation "for the one who fears God will follow both warnings"—i.e., both of the warnings in verses 16 and 17. But it is hard to see how this avoids the apparent moral relativism: just allow yourself a little bit (not too much) of righteousness *and* wickedness. And one might add that, without subsequent correction, 9:1–2 also seems to "encourage an antinomian rationalization of sin and moral compromise."

Verse 20 is the only verse of Ecclesiastes that is directly quoted in the New Testament.

> *Indeed, there is no one on earth who is righteous,*
>   *no one who does what is right and never sins. (7:20)*

Paul takes it as a statement of simple fact that stands in judgment upon every human being (Rom 3:10). In its context here, though, it sounds more like an excuse for the compromising ambiguity of verses 16–18. "Nobody is perfect, you see, so you might as well accommodate a bit of wickedness. You're inevitably going to sin some of the time. Just get over it." And then verses 21–22 seemingly add to that surrender by reminding us that any sin we condemn in others is probably true of ourselves.

> *21Do not pay attention to every word people say,*
>   *or you may hear your servant cursing you—*
> *22for you know in your heart*
>   *that many times you yourself have cursed others.*
>   *(7:21–22)*

Well, yes. But that's hardly a reason for indifference to crucial differences between righteousness and wickedness.

Conclusion of the Journey—So Far (7:23–29)

At this point, with these verses, we come to what seems to be the crux and central part of the whole book. We are not yet at the *climax* of the book, since that comes at the end. But we have reached a key moment, a halfway point on the journey.

> *23All this I tested by wisdom and I said,*
>
> > *"I am determined to be wise"—*
> >   *but this was beyond me.*

> [24]Whatever exists is far off and most profound—
>   who can discover it?
> [25]So I turned my mind to understand,
>   to investigate and to search out wisdom and the scheme
>   of things
> and to understand the stupidity of wickedness
>   and the madness of folly. (7:23–25)

Two important things emerge from this short passage.

- First, Qoheleth tells us just how hard he's been trying to find the answers he is looking for, but still thinks that, in spite of all his struggle, he has *failed* in that quest.
- Second, Qoheleth will come to a conclusion in verse 29, a conclusion that, in spite of all his negativity, shows us that he is still, somehow, a firm believer in the conflicting *double* truths of Genesis 1–3. Failure and faith stand side by side. Which is going to win?

Verses 23–25 are full of passionate and repetitive words. He has tried very hard indeed ("I am determined . . ."). He wants to *find* wisdom *by* wisdom! But in the end, he finds that wisdom is too far away and too deep.

But this is quite ironic. He is searching for wisdom and using wisdom to do so! It all seems a bit circular. And yet this is what we today might call the exercise of autonomous reason. Our rationality is a very good thing in itself—one of God's wonderful gifts to human creatures. And our rationality (our "wisdom") is outstandingly good at finding out the *causes* of things in a scientific sense. We can analyze and probe *backwards* into how things have come to be as they are. But the same rationality (on its own) is baffled when it comes to finding out the *meaning* of things, or the point and purpose of "life, the universe, and everything." Unaided human reason by itself cannot penetrate the meaning of the creation of which it is itself a part. We can explain *how* but can't explain *why*. We can uncover the *causes*, but we can't discern the *purpose*—not by ourselves.

And yet he has tried so hard! The first half of verse 25 uses three different words for intense mental effort (to understand, to investigate, and to search out). And all this struggle is to find "the scheme of things" (NIV), or better, "an *explanation*." The word *heshbon* means a "reckoning," the correct outcome of a complex equation, a satisfying conclusion after you've added everything together (as he uses the word in verse 27). It's rather like the ending of an Hercule Poirot mystery, when all loose ends are tied up, all clues explained, and the case is solved. That's the *heshbon* moment. But Qoheleth hasn't found any such satisfying explanatory conclusion in life, and he knows he won't find it in the grave—there will be no *heshbon* there (9:10).

The second half of verse 25 tells us one thing he particularly wants to know. *Why* is it stupid to be wicked? *Why* is it mad to be foolish? He surely believes, in both cases, that it *is*. But he can't *understand why* it should be so, and especially when he has provided plenty of empirical observation that points in the opposite direction. The wicked and the foolish seem to manage pretty well much of the time. And it could be said (it *does* get said) that it is actually more stupid and mad to spend your whole life trying to be righteous and wise if it gets you nowhere better in the end than those who are wicked and foolish. Round and round it goes in his head (and ours sometimes, if we're honest).

So what then has he found?

> *I find more bitter than death*
> *the woman who is a snare,*
> *whose heart is a trap*
> *and whose hands are chains.*
> *The man who pleases God will escape her,*
> *but the sinner she will ensnare. (7:26)*

At first glance, verse 26 sounds really rather trivial (at least in comparison with his "grand quest" for a solution to the mystery of life). Or, if you are a woman, it probably sounds downright insulting. Is this all he can do right now, just to warn us against prostitutes? Or is he just sounding off about women in general?

Is our Qoheleth actually a misogynist?

Well, possibly. Mind you, coming from the mouth of this "assumed" Solomon character, such an opinion would be even more ironic, given Solomon's excessive marital arrangements in which "the woman who is a snare" multiplied into hundreds of women in his harem. But even if Qoheleth has a misogynistic streak, and even if verses 26 and 28 are his personal experience of woman (unpleasantly derogatory), we must remember that we don't take his words as "gospel truth" any more than the words recorded of Job's friends. This is Qoheleth's own quest. This is *his* journey, *his* experience, *his* conclusion—not a revealed biblical truth!

However! There is another way of hearing verse 26, which I owe to Craig Bartholomew. He suggests that verse 26 may well be metaphorical. The "woman who is a snare" could well refer to Dame Folly, the seductive counterpoint to Lady Wisdom in Proverbs, the *femme fatale* who lures people into folly to their own harm.

Now, of course, the warnings in Proverbs are against *actual* sexual adultery and prostitution. It would be hard to take texts like Proverbs 5, 6, and 7 in any other way than as literally meant—a strong warning to avoid casual sex before or outside marriage, no matter what the enticements.

However, all through Proverbs 1–9 we are repeatedly urged to pay attention to a very binary choice: there are two ways to live, righteous or wicked, wise or foolish. There are two paths. There are two houses. And there are two *metaphorical* women. The climax of this opening and orienting section of Proverbs invites us to go and feast at the house of Lady Wisdom and enjoy all the benefits that she offers (Prov 9:1–12). But then we hear another voice, loud and beckoning. It is Dame Folly, calling "all who are simple . . . those who have no sense," who find her at first "sweet" and "delicious" but ultimately fatal (Prov 9:13–18).

So then, just as *wisdom* is personified in Proverbs as a worthy and wholesome woman who fosters healthy, righteous, and fulfilling life, so *folly* is personified as a dangerous woman whose enticements ultimately lead to sorrow and death. And, since Qoheleth's description of "the woman" in Ecclesiastes 7:26 uses very similar language to Proverbs, that may be his point. "The woman who is a snare" is the very folly he is struggling both to understand (v. 25) and to avoid.

But if that is so, then verse 26 may actually be a piece of harsh and despairing self-criticism. Qoheleth has struggled so hard to find *Wisdom* (the one "woman" he really wanted to find). But instead, all he has found is Dame *Folly*. He so desperately longed to embrace wisdom but has ended up in the arms of folly. He feels trapped in a vicious circle of deception from which he can't escape. And if he is only a sinner ensnared by folly (last line of v. 26), then his whole enterprise must be displeasing to God.

Indeed, one might ask, *where is God* in all this? Almost, but not quite, completely absent. A few moments ago, God was being accused of making things crooked, of making bad stuff as well as good stuff (7:13–14). What is lacking in this whole chapter so far in its restless searching for what is "good" is that essential ingredient of true wisdom, the fear of the Lord. Or at least, the kind of fear of the Lord that leads to a total commitment to righteous living and rejection of evil—not the eyebrow-raising apparent compromise and ambiguity of verse 18. The vital importance of true fear of the Lord will be reasserted before we finish the book, in chapter 12. But at this point, all Qoheleth is relying on is his own mental effort (v. 23).

Perhaps it is somewhat anachronistic to portray Qoheleth, as Bartholomew does, as operating with an "autonomous epistemology"—that is, seeking verifiable knowledge through empirical observation and reason alone, without recourse to divine revelation. But what does seem clear is that his determined but lonely search for wisdom is proving doubly frustrating. Not only has he *not* found what he is looking for, but arguably he *has* found only the folly he knows is a snare. There is a great deal of irony and tragedy in this quest. There are times Qoheleth sounds like Nietzsche at his most despairingly cynical and teasingly aphoristic.

Perhaps the author of the book, the Frame-Narrator of the opening and closing sections, realizes just how shocking and confusing are the conclusions being offered in these verses. So he interjects in verse 27 a reminder that he is only reporting the words of Qoheleth ("says the Teacher"), which he will "adjust" later. We need to remember this is the story of Qoheleth's quest.

And that quest still seems pretty hopeless when we read verse 28.

> *while I was still searching*
> *but not finding—*
> *I found one upright man among a thousand,*
> *but not one upright woman among them all. (7:28)*

Are we back with the misogynist flavor of verse 26 (if read literally)?

Before we jump to that conclusion, remember that the whole thrust of this section is on *searching but not finding*. So this comment is not a mere digression into a derogatory comparison between men and women. The point is, he simply can't find what he's looking for, and *nobody* seems able to help, whether male or female. The word "man" is *'adam*, the general word for human beings, not *'ish*—for a male. And the word "upright" (NIV) is not in the Hebrew at all (cf. ESV). It is imported from verse 29. Furthermore, verse 28b is in the form of Hebrew parallelism. That is, it is making a *single* point through a pair of lines, not two separate points. He means that in all his searching it was hard to find even one person in a thousand (to do what? to explain the meaning of life?). So it is hardly complimentary to men and insulting to women to say, "I found 0.1 percent of men and 0.0 percent of women able to help my search." His point is: *nobody* could help me find the answers I wanted.

Eugene Peterson sees it this way in *The Message*: "The wisdom I've looked for I haven't found. I didn't find one man or woman in a thousand worth my while." In the light of the whole thrust of the passage since verse 23, that seems a better interpretation than to assume he is telling us, rather tangentially, that women have always disappointed him—though that of course is entirely possible for this character.

But suddenly the chapter ends with a surprising flash of insight, which seems to counteract some of the pessimism of the preceding verses, and especially the moral confusion of verses 13–18.

> *This only have I found:*
> *God created mankind upright,*
> *but they have gone in search of many schemes. (7:29)*

In fact, he starts this verse quite emphatically, "Only—Look!—*this* I have found. . . ." NIV leaves out "Look!" but it sounds like Qoheleth wants to catch our attention and urge us to accept what he is now about to say. After all his fruitless searching, there is indeed something ("*This!*") that he has come to realize, and it quite radically changes some earlier disappointments. So, "Look here, this is important. . . ."

Ecclesiastes 7:29 is short, but it packs Genesis 1–2 and 3 into a single verse: the goodness of God's original creation and the spoiling "schemes" of humanity.

There is a rather clever pun here, with two Hebrew words that sound very similar:

- *Heshbon*, which we saw above means *an explanation*, the rationale that he was looking for.

- *Hishebonoth*, which means *schemes, inventions* (such as war machines, 2 Chr 26:15).

So this second word speaks of inventions of our own devising, human cleverness employed for evil purposes since the fall.

This assertion in 7:29 simply contradicts the opinion we heard in 7:13—"Everything is bent, and it's all God's doing." No, Qoheleth now realizes, everything, including the human race, was good when God made it, but we've messed things up ourselves. We can't blame God for the catastrophe we brought on ourselves.

When God looks at the human race, he could be wearing that T-shirt that people in Belfast wear. Belfast (my native city) is home of the famous shipyard that built the doomed *Titanic*. On the T-shirt, underneath a picture of the great ship, comes the disclaimer, "She was fine when she left here!" (which you need to say with a good strong Belfast accent). A touch of dark humor, but about a reality that is not funny at all, either for the *Titanic* or the human race. We were fine, is the point, when we first left God's hands.

So Qoheleth has reached a crucial and penetrating awareness. He now at least understands where the cause of his baffled incomprehension lies, and it is not with God. He realizes why he cannot fathom the meaning of life by human wisdom alone, why there's a world he cannot understand. The reason lies in human sinfulness and fallen inventiveness.

In desiring the "knowledge of good and evil" (in the story of Gen 3), we sought to take control of our own "moral compass." We thought we could define for ourselves what is right and wrong, wise and foolish, and we ended up in the utter moral, spiritual, and intellectual mess we are in. We cannot find the truth about the world apart from the revelation of God. To try to do so is inherently a form of idolatry—worship of ourselves, our own rationality, our own competence.

And in this realization we find some clue that can help toward bridging that chasm that runs through the whole book, the chasm between his dominant theme of the meaninglessness of so much that he sees in the world around him and his repeated affirmation of the goodness of life and the creation gifts of God. The biblical narrative recognizes that chasm and puts it into proper perspective, even if not providing neat explanations for every absurdity. The great drama of Scripture began with Act 1, God's good creation, but moved on to Act 2, humanity's sinful rebellion. That's what Qoheleth summarizes in 7:29. There are still struggles ahead on his journey, but at least he is now getting the start of the biblical story right. And that is a crucially important beginning—for him and for all of us. We won't make sense of the rest of the Bible's story, or allow it to inject its sense into the enigmas of Ecclesiastes, unless we grasp the truth of that story's beginnings. Ecclesiastes 7:29 is a foundational recognition.

Well, as we proceed into chapters 8 and 9, we'll find that this valid insight at the end of chapter 7 does not provide much comfort by itself. He still has to live in a world he cannot understand and die in a way he cannot predict or avoid. Nevertheless, *it is a truth*—a biblical truth—and he has articulated it succinctly and truthfully. So that is at least a good foundation. "Facts are our friends," as one of my working colleagues repeatedly tells us, even when we don't like them!

Indeed, even this limited perspective holds some hope. For if we were upright once, might we not become so again? A story that did not begin with our *rebellion*, but with our *creation*, holds out possibilities—if our Creator God so chooses (and he does!). Derek Kidner puts it perfectly:

> After the gropings of this chapter, this verse [7:29] brings refreshing certainty that our *many devices*—our clouding of moral issues, our refusal of the straight way—are our fault, not our fate. . . . Since futility was not the first word about our world, it no longer has to be the last.[4]

---

4. Derek Kidner, *The Message of Ecclesiastes: A Time to Mourn and a Time to Dance*, The Bible Speaks Today (Leicester: Inter-Varsity Press, 1976), 73.

LIFE IS INEXPLICABLE (8:1–17)

After the roller coaster of chapter 7, we are back in somewhat familiar territory now, as chapter 8:1 signals with its rather straightforward praise of wisdom—though such praise comes now somewhat sullied by the more pessimistic ponderings of chapter 7. That is immediately followed by some more observations about social and political life, about which (as we've seen already) Qoheleth is more than a little cynical and suspicious.

Negotiating Tyranny (8:1–9)

Political life is ambiguous and can be threatening. These verses seem like a litany of rather pragmatic advice to anyone in public office.

> *²Obey the king's command, I say, because you took an oath before God. ³Do not be in a hurry to leave the king's presence. Do not stand up for a bad cause, for he will do whatever he pleases. ⁴Since a king's word is supreme, who can say to him, "What are you doing?"*
>
> > *⁵Whoever obeys his command will come to no harm,*
> >   *and the wise heart will know the proper time and procedure.*
> > *⁶For there is a proper time and procedure for every matter,*
> >   *though a person may be weighed down by misery.*
> >
> > *⁷Since no one knows the future,*
> >   *who can tell someone else what is to come?*
> > *⁸As no one has power over the wind to contain it,*
> >   *so no one has power over the time of their death.*
> > *As no one is discharged in time of war,*
> >   *so wickedness will not release those who practice it.*
>
> *⁹All this I saw, as I applied my mind to everything done under the sun. There is a time when a man lords it over others to his own hurt. (8:2–9)*

If you are in some administrative post as part of the government machinery, you may find that you have to do things that, for personal or ethical reasons, you would normally avoid. But because of your oath that you took before God to show loyalty to the head of government (whether king, president, prime minister, or whatever), you will have to submit to that higher human authority (v. 2). You will face uncomfortable clashes between your conscience and your political allegiance—a dilemma of faith and political loyalty that afflicts Christians in politics still.

And whatever your personal standing as an advisor to the head of government, remember who is the boss. He will do whatever he wants anyway, so your choices are tough. And he may rule autocratically, unaccountable to anyone and accepting no criticism (vv. 3–4).

The wisest course in most circumstances is to go along with your instructions, use your discretion and common sense, and hope for the best but prepare for the worst (vv. 5–6).

And since nothing in life is certain, except death, politics is intrinsically unpredictable, except that wickedness will catch up with you in the end. So all in all, politics brings tough decisions and unseen dangers. When anybody exercises power over others, people get hurt—sometimes the one wielding the power (vv. 7–9).

Protesting Injustice (8:10–15)

Meanwhile, life just goes on being absurdly unfair.

> [10] Then too, I saw the wicked buried—those who used to come and go from the holy place and receive praise in the city where they did this. This too is meaningless.
>
> [11] When the sentence for a crime is not quickly carried out, people's hearts are filled with schemes to do wrong. [12] Although a wicked person who commits a hundred crimes may live a long time, I know that it will go better with those who fear God, who are reverent before him. [13] Yet because the wicked do not fear God,

it will not go well with them, and their days will not lengthen like a shadow.

¹⁴There is something else meaningless that occurs on earth: the righteous who get what the wicked deserve, and the wicked who get what the righteous deserve. This too, I say, is meaningless. (8:10–14)

Verse 10 is somewhat unclear. It might mean that the wicked get praise during their lifetime, even in the places where they carried out their wickedness. And we all know that people have such short memories and fickle allegiance, especially in the political realm. The latest news story quickly displaces awareness of faults and failings even in the recent past. Or it might mean that praise is lavished on the wicked after their death, even when everybody knows they were scoundrels. Hypocrisy rules.

Verse 11 anticipates an English proverb that "delayed justice is no justice" and only encourages increased wrongdoing.

At first sight, verses 12 and 13 seem mutually contradictory:

- v. 12—the wicked *may* live a long time (but it will be better for the righteous in the end);
- v. 13—the wicked will *not* live long (since they don't fear God).

Well, which is it? Probably verse 13 is what he wishes were true, while verse 12 expresses what he sees happening. But either way (and this is the important point), Qoheleth tells us that this is something that he "*knows*" (he emphasizes the word in verse 12). So here we have strong affirmation of his underlying faith. In spite of some of the things he has said before (and will muse over again later), he has this deep-down certainty that ultimately the fate of the righteous and the wicked will be different. The fear of the Lord—present or absent—is the determining factor.

BUT, then, in his typical way, having stated what he knows

and affirms by faith ("that it will go better with those who fear God"), he immediately contrasts it with the baffling enigma that this distinction can seem to be reversed in real life (v. 14). And this seems just plain meaningless—he puts the word at the beginning and end of the verse.

And we have to agree with him, don't we? It seems not just pointless but downright unfair, unjust, absurd, and unbearable when good people get treated like criminals while actual criminals get off scot-free. We cry out in protest, "Why?" And if that is our *human* instinct, Proverbs tells us that it stinks in God's nostrils also.

> Acquitting the guilty and condemning the innocent—
> the LORD detests them both. (Prov 17:15)

Of course, Qoheleth could not have seen that, eventually, it would be the supreme historical instance of what Ecclesiastes 8:14a describes that would ultimately remove the "meaninglessness." For that line, "the righteous who get what the wicked deserve" is exactly what happened at the cross of Christ. That is where "God made him who had no sin to be sin for us, so that in him we might become the righteousness of God" (2 Cor 5:21). The ultimate *human injustice* of the cross became the ultimate *divine justice* on our behalf in the saving, reconciling righteousness of God.

Qoheleth, of course, is not thinking of that astonished vision of the prophet:

> [4]Surely he took up our pain
>   and bore our suffering,
> yet we considered him punished by God,
>   stricken by him, and afflicted.
> [5]But he was pierced for our transgressions,
>   he was crushed for our iniquities;
> the punishment that brought us peace was on him,
>   and by his wounds we are healed.

⁶We all, like sheep, have gone astray,
 each of us has turned to our own way;
and the LORD has laid on him
 the iniquity of us all. (Isa 53:4–6)

For Qoheleth, verse 14 simply summarizes the absurdity and unfairness of this life. Bad people and good people often get the opposite of what they deserve.

And yet! Still he bounces back with yet another of his strong affirmations of the goodness of life—the fifth in fact,

¹⁵So I commend the enjoyment of life, because there is nothing better for a person under the sun than to eat and drink and be glad. Then joy will accompany them in their toil all the days of the life God has given them under the sun. (8:15)

This one is short, but it carries the same message. Food, drink, joy, work . . . these are all good things. So "I commend them," he says. "Enjoy them," he says.

But, we protest in amazement, how can you possibly commend verse 15 straight after observing verse 14? How can you enjoy life in a world so full of absurd injustice? Is there not a glaring moral contradiction here? And if that contradiction is obvious to us, it can't be merely accidental, as if Qoheleth couldn't see the clash between the meaninglessness of verse 14 and the commendation of verse 15.

Qoheleth seems to be deliberately putting side by side two diametrically opposite ways of looking at life that we nevertheless have to live with somehow:

- Life is full of meaningless injustice (v. 14).
- Life is all about enjoying the good gifts of God (v. 15).

They might seem contradictory, and yet he has to state them both as true—one as a truth of empirical observation, the other as a truth of scriptural faith. He cannot deny the first without denying the eyes in his own head. And he cannot deny the second without denying the faith that is the foundation of his whole worldview.

This combination reminds me of the song that a small community of believers in Costa Rica sing before every meal. Casa Adobe is an intentional and creative small community of people, led and hosted by Ruth and Jim Padilla DeBorst. It is a community that includes some needy and broken people—casualties of a broken world. Yet they live and share together, and in their meals they very consciously *celebrate and enjoy* God's gifts of wholesome food and good wine. Their grace before meals (which I have sung with them on a short stay there some years ago) acknowledges the dual reality of our text: the goodness of God's creation gift of bread and the presence of hunger and injustice in our world. An English translation of the Spanish goes like this:

> Bless, O Lord, this our bread.
> Give bread to those who are hungry,
> And hunger for justice to those who have bread.
> Bless, O Lord, this our bread.

It is a thoroughly biblical combination of gratitude and lament.

Debunking Arrogance (8:16–17)

Coming back to Qoheleth, he concludes this chapter with characteristic bafflement. Even with the exhaustion of comprehensive study and inquiry—day and night—he cannot find what he's looking for.

> [16]*When I applied my mind to know wisdom and to observe the labor that is done on earth—people getting no sleep day or night—*[17]*then I saw all that God has done. No one can comprehend what goes on under the sun. Despite all their efforts to search it out, no one*

can discover its meaning. Even if the wise claim they know, they cannot really comprehend it. (8:16–17)

He reminds us of the task that has occupied him since the beginning of the book—a comprehensive study of "the labor that is done on earth" (v. 16), or as he put it in 1:13, "all that is done under the heavens." And it is clear that he is referring to the vast enterprise of humanity, all our human works, accomplishments, and the great wonders of civilization.

But we might well query the way, in verse 17, he seems to equate that great *human* effort with "all that *God* has done." Surely God's work on earth exceeds all that *mankind* has done. What about creation itself? What about the great acts of judgment and redemption in Israel's grand narrative?

Perhaps we are being too critical, but we can at least admire his *humility*: he knows that he can't understand the whole meaning of life, no matter how hard he tries. He is not claiming, in 8:1a, that the wise have *all* the explanations for *everything*. And we can smile at his *honesty* as he pricks the bubble of academic arrogance: he knows that nobody else can fully understand it all either, no matter what they claim! There is a world out there that *he* can't understand. Perhaps it's just a crumb of bleak comfort that he realizes that he's not the only one.

DEATH IS INESCAPABLE (9:1–12)

This chapter is probably the most starkly negative of the whole book, coming just before the final section. And yet, amazingly it also contains the most positive of all the life affirmations. It is a chapter of immense, yawning contrasts.

Death Destroys Everything (9:1–6)

Qoheleth has faced up to death several times already. He is baffled and distressed about it because it seems to destroy the whole point of life no matter what you achieve. And in any case, you can't control what comes after you, so any hopes of a great legacy are very vulnerable.

Here he goes even further. Death seems to destroy even some distinctions that are an essential part of biblical faith.

> *¹So I reflected on all this and concluded that the righteous and the wise and what they do are in God's hands, but no one knows whether love or hate awaits them. ²All share a common destiny—the righteous and the wicked, the good and the bad, the clean and the unclean, those who offer sacrifices and those who do not.*
>
> > *As it is with the good,*
> >   *so with the sinful;*
> > *as it is with those who take oaths,*
> >   *so with those who are afraid to take them.*
>
> *³This is the evil in everything that happens under the sun: The same destiny overtakes all. The hearts of people, moreover, are full of evil and there is madness in their hearts while they live, and afterward they join the dead. ⁴Anyone who is among the living has hope—even a live dog is better off than a dead lion!*
>
> > *⁵For the living know that they will die,*
> >   *but the dead know nothing;*
> > *they have no further reward,*
> >   *and even their name is forgotten.*
> > *⁶Their love, their hate*
> >   *and their jealousy have long since vanished;*
> > *never again will they have a part*
> >   *in anything that happens under the sun. (9:1–6)*

The chapter opens with a statement that is as shocking as any we have come across anywhere so far. Qoheleth starts by affirming a core element in any believer's theology, a conviction that is repeatedly held out as a massively comforting security in the books of Psalms and Proverbs. That statement of faith is that if you follow the Bible's teaching, fear God, and live in a way that is righteous and wise, then your life is safe in the hands of God (1a). Agreed?

But then, in the second half of verse 1 he slams in a real jaw-dropper. That may be all very well in life (though even that is questionable, as he has pointed out in 8:14), but what happens when you die? What good is your righteousness and wisdom then? What "awaits" you on the other side of death?

"Love or hate" stands here for God's approval or God's judgment. Which will it be? Nobody knows! Nobody has come back to tell us. "As far as the eye can see," as it were, it's the same for everybody! Death is our common destiny, and what lies beyond death might be the same for everybody too. We just don't know.

Can he really mean this?

Yes, and he rubs it in further in verse 2.

Take a close look at all the contrasting pairs of words Qoheleth lists in this verse.

- Righteous and wicked
- Good and bad
- Clean and unclean
- Those who sacrifice and those who do not
- Good people and sinners
- Oath-takers and non-oath-takers

These are critical distinctions. They are like polar opposites in Israel's covenant faith. And since Qoheleth is obviously an Israelite believer in Yahweh, he is familiar with these distinctions that underlie the whole narrative and fabric of the Torah.

He knows the faith he is subjecting to the acid test of death. Here is his list of clear and stark distinctions that he knew from the Scriptures. These were some of the very criteria of God's approval or judgment.

But, he contends, none of these opposites makes any difference in the end! Death collapses all such distinctions into meaningless equivalence. Whether you have lived on one side of these binaries or the other doesn't matter. When you're dead, you're dead, and we all end up in the same state—whatever that might be.

Now of course, as we've learned to accept from this writer, Qoheleth cheerfully contradicts himself as he wrestles with the mysteries of life and death, trying so hard to reconcile the tensions they throw up. Remember how, back in 5:1–7, he warned us to be thoughtful and careful in how we worship and to be cautious in what we promise with vows or oaths? But here he suggests that it doesn't really matter anyway. All your religious practices and sworn commitments will make no difference. You will end up just as dead either way, and nobody knows what your fate will be. "The same destiny overtakes all" (v. 3).

Death, then, is simply an inexplicable evil and as unacceptable as madness. It is the evil end to the evil hearts of evil people while we live in this evil world (v. 3). Qoheleth at least takes very seriously the verdict on human life that we read in texts like these:

> The LORD saw how great the wickedness of the human race had become on the earth, and that every inclination of the thoughts of the human heart was only evil all the time. (Gen 6:5)

> The heart is deceitful above all things
> and beyond cure.
> Who can understand it? (Jer 17:9)

What's that you say?

"But surely it's better to be alive than dead, even if you're only a live dog!" (see v. 4).

Well, yes, maybe so. But it's only "better" because when you're alive at least you know you're going to die, but when you're dead, you'll know nothing at all (v. 5a)!

Verses 5–6 are shatteringly negative and pessimistic. Death seems to rule out any value in life. Death abruptly terminates all our relationships, whether good or bad, all our emotions and passions, all our participation in the world of the living.

This seems to be the end of the road for Qoheleth's quest, or at least one dimension of it. He simply cannot *see* beyond death. And since his whole quest is based on what he can *see*, he cannot see any value in a life that has to be lived with the constant prospect of death. He appears to end up in almost total nihilism.

Yet once again we have to detect an element of irony here. There is something that Qoheleth actually knows, even if he doesn't see its implications. For he boldly declares, "*This is the evil . . .*" (v. 3). But where does that evaluation come from? If *everything* is ultimately meaningless and indistinguishable—then how can he say that one thing is evil rather than another? The very idea of something being evil and another thing being good comes from some objectively real standard that must transcend our own limited lives and experience. Otherwise, how would we know? *Knowing that evil is evil*, and being capable of morally evaluating it as such, requires an awareness of the alternative and some objective grounds for making the distinction.

Even our sense of outrage at the evilness of evil (which is so characteristic of Qoheleth), is a sign of hope. Protest only makes sense when it emerges from a longing for a reality that one knows to be good. Protest against evil, on the assumption that it *is* evil, shows that we know there could and should be something *better*. We only know what is evil because we know what is good. And because we know the difference, we long for there to be something *better* than what we see around us.

But *will* there ever be?

Will there ever be anything better than this world with all its infuriating absurdities?

The answer to that question can only lie with God. But even when we believe that God does have the answer to the problem of evil, injustice, and death itself, we might remain as baffled as Qoheleth, *unless and until we take the wider Bible story into account.* And we shall do that a bit later.

Life Is a Gift and a Joy (9:7–10)

> *7Go, eat your food with gladness, and drink your wine with a joyful heart, for God has already approved what you do. 8Always be clothed in white, and always anoint your head with oil. 9Enjoy life with your wife, whom you love, all the days of this meaningless life that God has given you under the sun—all your meaningless days. For this is your lot in life and in your toilsome labor under the sun. 10Whatever your hand finds to do, do it with all your might, for in the realm of the dead, where you are going, there is neither working nor planning nor knowledge nor wisdom. (9:7–10)*

We are getting so used to this tactic by now! Against the utterly bleak background of verses 1–6, Qoheleth comes out yet again with his strong affirmation of the goodness of life here and now. Of course, we're all going to die! But nevertheless, life is to be enjoyed as God's gift in the meantime. In fact, the prospect of inevitable death makes this all the more urgent and imperative. Enjoy life before it's too late!

We hear again, for the sixth time, his summons to enjoy life. And this time it is as full and unreserved as it gets, though with some negative sarcasm so typical of his dark humor. But what an astonishing paradox it is that Qoheleth is able to gush with the sentiments of verses 7–10 after wallowing in the misery of verses 1–6!

With strong emphasis (notice how he invokes God twice), he advocates, or rather, he *commands* us to enjoy:

- Food and drink
- Joyful hearts
- Bright clothing
- Oil (scented perfume)
- Marriage
- Work

And we should enjoy all these things as heartily as we can—while we are alive. For of course in the grave we will have none of them. That at least is a spur to living life to the full now. For some people it's the only one. And even for the Christian, it's a powerful one as far as it goes. We do indeed have only limited time to serve God and enjoy his gifts in our earthly lifetime, even though we know much more about what lies beyond death than Qoheleth could have. So we should live as enthusiastically and productively as we can while we can. There is a perfectly proper kind of Christian opportunism, in view of the shortness of our life on earth.

> [4]As long as it is day, we must do the works of him who sent me. Night is coming, when no one can work. (John 9:4)

> [15]Be very careful, then, how you live—not as unwise but as wise, [16]making the most of every opportunity, because the days are evil. (Eph 5:15–16)

> [21]For to me, to live is Christ and to die is gain. [22]If I am to go on living in the body, this will mean fruitful labor for me. (Phil 1:21–22)

But what is going on here, as we sense Qoheleth trying to hold together verses 1–6 with verses 7–10? We can feel an enormous tension. There is a tug-of-war going on in Qoheleth's mind. And it is between these two things:

- **What he observes: Life is meaningless.** This is the logical implication of his epistemology—all he can see with empirical tools; life is rendered apparently pointless by death.
- **What he believes: Life is good.** This is the orthodox creation-faith of Israel: life is good in so many ways because it is the gift of the one, true, good, and living Lord God.

These two perspectives are pulling each other apart. And they are pulling Qoheleth apart like an unresolvable tension in his mind. His quest seems to be leading him to radical dichotomy—two opposite interpretations of life that seem to contradict and cancel each other, and there seems to be no way to bridge the gap. Indeed, the negativity of what he observes seems to creep into the positive affirmation that he wants to make on the basis of his creation-faith. So even the joy of marriage is only for "all your meaningless days" (v. 9b). And even the satisfaction of hard and fulfilling work is tainted with the prospect of no meaningful work at all after death (v. 10b).

So even in the midst of this, his sixth and longest life affirmation, his intuition of the meaninglessness and transience of it all tugs away at his joy in life. How can one bridge the gap between the sheer goodness and joy of life and the despairing enigmas of death? Even the remarkable insight of 7:29 has not prevented this climactic and unresolved tension. It begins to feel like Qoheleth, at this point of his quest, could join U2 in the repeated refrain of one of their most poignant songs, "I still haven't found what I'm looking for."[5]

Life Is Unpredictable: Death Is Unavoidable (9:11–12)

Qoheleth returns to the matter of unpredictability. First of all comes a typically brilliant piece of poetry. It is sharp, brief, simple, concrete—and true! It packs a powerful point: that you can never

---

5. From their album, *The Joshua Tree*, Island Records, 1987.

be certain of any outcome, no matter how obvious it might seem in advance by all appearances.

> [11] *I have seen something else under the sun:*
>
>> *The race is not to the swift*
>>> *or the battle to the strong,*
>> *nor does food come to the wise*
>>> *or wealth to the brilliant*
>> *or favor to the learned;*
>>> *but time and chance happen to them all.* (9:11)

By the way, I love how George Orwell "translates" this into the kind of modern English he so much deplored. This is in his classic essay, "Politics and the English Language," where he argues for simple language with plain words rather than fancy polysyllabic and pretentious jargon. Praising Ecclesiastes for its powerful and concrete simplicity, he parodies how this verse would be expressed today.

> Objective considerations of contemporary phenomenon compel the conclusion that success or failure in competitive activities exhibits no tendency to be commensurate with innate capacity, but that a considerable element of the unpredictable must be invariably taken into account.[6]

Well, quite! Give me Qoheleth any day!

But there is a deeper point to Qoheleth's observation. It qualifies one of the recurrent themes in the book of Proverbs, namely the "character-consequence" principle. That is, the oft-repeated admonition that, for example, if you work hard you will prosper;

---

6. George Orwell, "Politics and the English Language," first published in *Horizon* 13:76 (April 1946), 252–65.

if you are lazy, you'll sink into poverty.[7] Qoheleth says, "Not always, as far as I can see." And he was right, of course.

Qoheleth forces us to realize that we can't take the generalized principles of Proverbs as unexceptionable laws or as cast-iron promises. Biblical faith does not have a mechanical view of the universe. There are indeed moral principles and consequences built into the universe as God has ordained it. But life throws up all kinds of exceptions when things don't work out as we thought they should. Wisdom takes account of *both* dimensions of life: the general principles and the absurd exceptions.

And on top of that, our own death is unpredictable as to *when* it will happen, though it is utterly certain *that* it will.

> *Moreover, no one knows when their hour will come:*
>
> > *As fish are caught in a cruel net,*
> > *or birds are taken in a snare,*
> > *so people are trapped by evil times*
> > *that fall unexpectedly upon them. (9:12)*

Evil things like death itself come like a net to a fish or a snare to a bird—unexpected but unavoidable once you've been trapped. Christians are not exempt from such "evil times." They happen. The challenge for us who are in Christ is to know how to "stand" in the evil day:

> Therefore put on the full armor of God, so that when the day of evil comes, you may be able to stand your ground, and after you have done everything, to stand. (Eph 6:13)

Life, then, is unpredictable, even with all the best principles of wisdom in place; and death is inevitable and unavoidable.

---

7. E.g., Prov 6:6–11; 12:24, 27; 24:30–34; 28:19.

QUESTIONING WISDOM (9:13–16)[8]

> [13]*I also saw under the sun this example of wisdom that greatly impressed me:* [14]*There was once a small city with only a few people in it. And a powerful king came against it, surrounded it and built huge siege works against it.* [15]*Now there lived in that city a man poor but wise, and he saved the city by his wisdom. But nobody remembered that poor man.* [16]*So I said, "Wisdom is better than strength." But the poor man's wisdom is despised, and his words are no longer heeded. (9:13–16)*

This little story seems to be told merely to reinforce the point that even an example of good wisdom working well gets forgotten and despised. An example of wisdom (which may refer to some well-known historical event that Qoheleth's own contemporaries would have recognized) turns out to show that even wisdom has no lasting value and may not even be remembered. And somehow, after a chapter like this, we could be forgiven for thinking, "Well, what else would you expect? That's this world for you."

QUESTIONS FOR REFLECTION OR DISCUSSION

1. Ecclesiastes 7:1–10 lists several paradoxes, where something negative can be surprisingly "better" than its opposite (when you think about it). Have you found other examples in your own experience where that is true to life? Has it led you to a better conclusion than Qoheleth offers in 7:14?
2. In the light of Qoheleth's words about the tensions and dangers of political life in 8:1–9, can you identify and discuss some current issues in which Christians involved in public and political life have to cope with conflict between their principles and the circumstances surrounding them?

---

8. 9:17–18, pointing out that good advice is all very well, but "one sinner" can muck it all up, probably belongs to the sequence of proverbs in chapter 10.

3. Discuss your reactions to Qoheleth's brutal frankness about death in 9:1–6 (please be sensitive as you do so to any bereaved members of your group). Do you find it:
   ○ Refreshingly honest?
   ○ Repellingly insensitive?
   ○ True, but not the whole truth?

CHAPTER 5

REJOICE AND REMEMBER!

Ecclesiastes 9:17–12:14

Finally, we reach the end of Qoheleth's quest (he closes with his poem in 12:1–7), and then comes the concluding verdict and advice of the Frame-Narrator (12:8–14). In the end they agree—mostly! The Frame-Narrator will compliment Qoheleth (12:9–10), but his own final words do contradict, or at least put under severe criticism, some of Qoheleth's more radically negative ponderings that have shocked us from time to time. In the end, the Frame-Narrator affirms those faith-based convictions that Qoheleth also held, rather than allowing his "meaninglessness" texts to prevail. However, as we shall see, that does not mean that either Qoheleth or the Frame-Narrator think they have cheerfully solved the whole problem. No, the brute observable fact of *hebel* remains (12:8). There is still so much about life in this world that is baffling, enigmatic, and seemingly pointless. We live in a world where so much happens that simply defies rational explanation. Faith does not *deny* the struggles of life but summons us to live with God in the midst of them—even without satisfying explanations and answers.

"TWO WAYS TO LIVE": WISDOM OR FOLLY? YES, BUT . . . (9:17–11:6)

This section feels like a calm interlude, giving us a pause for breath after the searing negativity of chapter 9, before we move on to the more positive concluding passages.

Remember that Qoheleth stands in the tradition of Israel's wisdom literature. He belonged among "the wise" (12:9–11). And running through that whole tradition is a fundamental duality: wisdom or folly. You have to choose. And Israel's faith, of course, urges us to choose the first.

Indeed, we can point out some other key dimensions to this duality. At least three fundamental opposites are constantly put before our eyes in the wisdom tradition.

- Wise   Foolish
- Righteous   Wicked
- Godly   Ungodly[1]

This means that Israel's wisdom teachers saw a strong connection between the *intellectual, moral, and spiritual* dimensions of human life. They all impact each other. The Israelites did not split apart academic learning, ethical behavior, and religious faith.

That is why the fear of the Lord is the first principle of wisdom. We need to know what to *believe* (which comes from knowing whom to *trust*). And that is foundational for then knowing how to *think* (because God shapes our whole worldview and mental categories). And on the basis of that combination of God-focused faith and reason, we will then know how to *behave*. And it is in our relationship with the living God (in the fear of the Lord) that we receive God's guidance in all three areas. The fear of the Lord will shape our lives into the ways of wisdom, righteousness, and godliness and help us to avoid their opposites, the ways of folly, wickedness, and ungodliness.

Now, Qoheleth knows and broadly accepts that worldview. And he knows many proverbs that express it, such as we find in abundance in the book of Proverbs. But he cannot help

---

1. All three polarities are abundantly emphasized in Proverbs 1–9, which stands as a theological and ethical prologue for the rest of the book.

commenting, even here, that observation of life often seems to undermine those simple binary opposites or show that things can be more complicated and uncertain than those polarities suggest. And so there is confusion and enigma still, even when we accept the basic affirmations of wisdom, righteousness, and godliness.

Accordingly, in 9:17–11:6 he gives us a mixture of traditional proverbs that mostly reflect that "two-ways" worldview. But then he sets alongside them a number of comments (his own "alternative facts," we might say) that force us to hang a few question marks around what seems obvious or certain. Life just doesn't always work out like it's supposed to.

We know which of the "two ways" we ought to choose. We strive to choose the way of wisdom, righteousness, and godliness.

Yes, but—sometimes . . .

Sometimes Folly Rules (9:17–10:7)

> ¹⁷*The quiet words of the wise are more to be heeded*
> *than the shouts of a ruler of fools.*
> ¹⁸*Wisdom is better than weapons of war,*
> *but one sinner destroys much good.*
> ^{10:1}*As dead flies give perfume a bad smell,*
> *so a little folly outweighs wisdom and honor.*
> ²*The heart of the wise inclines to the right,*
> *but the heart of the fool to the left.*
> ³*Even as fools walk along the road,*
> *they lack sense*
> *and show everyone how stupid they are.*
> ⁴*If a ruler's anger rises against you,*
> *do not leave your post;*
> *calmness can lay great offenses to rest.*
>
> ⁵*There is an evil I have seen under the sun,*
> *the sort of error that arises from a ruler:*
> ⁶*Fools are put in many high positions,*

> *while the rich occupy the low ones.*
> *⁷I have seen slaves on horseback,*
>   *while princes go on foot like slaves. (9:17–10:7)*

We begin with an obvious truth in verses 17–18a, on which we'd all agree. But then the truth of 18b and 10:1 is equally obvious. "There's always one!" we say, when some idiot (we think) messes up everybody else's good work. So much wisdom and patience can be destroyed by one stupid action, or one daft fool, one hurtful or confidence-breaking word, or one lying politician. . . .

Right and left (vv. 2–3) are clear binary opposites, illustrating the "two ways." And the fool is somebody who habitually chooses the wrong one and shows everybody what a fool he or she is. Once again, we can all nod in agreement.

But then, things may not be so clear in the political world. Even if "Keep Calm and Carry On" sounds like good advice (v. 4), we may end up being governed by fools (vv. 5–6)—and how true that sounds in today's world in several countries. And a mere reversal of the system (perhaps by revolution) may only pile absurdity on top of injustice (v. 7). And there are modern examples of that too.

So, we may all agree on the benefits of standard wisdom. But when folly comes to dominate the key levers of life, you see some pretty strange and unwelcome sights.

Sometimes Accidents Happen (10:8–15)

> *⁸Whoever digs a pit may fall into it;*
>   *whoever breaks through a wall may be bitten by*
>   *a snake.*
> *⁹Whoever quarries stones may be injured by them;*
>   *whoever splits logs may be endangered by them.*
>
> *¹⁰If the axe is dull*
>   *and its edge unsharpened,*

more strength is needed,
  but skill will bring success.

[11] If a snake bites before it is charmed,
  the charmer receives no fee.

[12] Words from the mouth of the wise are gracious,
  but fools are consumed by their own lips.
[13] At the beginning their words are folly;
  at the end they are wicked madness—
    [14] and fools multiply words.

No one knows what is coming—
  who can tell someone else what will happen after them?

[15] The toil of fools wearies them;
  they do not know the way to town. (10:8–15)

Verse 8 is a traditional proverb stating the law of "acts and consequences." Digging a pit was probably a metaphor for planning evil. Breaking through meant burglary of someone else's house. But the proverb warns that both may rebound on the perpetrator with unforeseen disaster to themselves. Some kind of punishment will follow the crime, even if not delivered by a judge in court.

But then the following verses seem to imply that unforeseen bad consequences don't follow only *bad* actions. Even doing *good* ordinary jobs that are perfectly legitimate (v. 9) can lead to accidental injury too, which is not at all deserved. And even expertise, though it can lead to success, won't necessarily save you from harm; things can always go wrong, sometimes fatally (vv. 10–11).

Verses 12–15 all sound like good common sense, with a touch of humor in verse 15 (the fool can't even find his way home!). But in the middle of the familiar proverbial observations, we suddenly get a flash of Qoheleth's familiar caustic realism. We really don't know what's coming round the next bend to hit us (like a flying stone or axe-head, v. 9) or what will happen after we've gone (v. 14b). Stuff happens. Get over it.

Sometimes Money Talks (10:16–20)

¹⁶*Woe to the land whose king was a servant*
and whose princes feast in the morning.
¹⁷*Blessed is the land whose king is of noble birth*
and whose princes eat at a proper time—
for strength and not for drunkenness.

¹⁸*Through laziness, the rafters sag;*
because of idle hands, the house leaks.

¹⁹*A feast is made for laughter,*
wine makes life merry,
and money is the answer for everything.

²⁰*Do not revile the king even in your thoughts,*
or curse the rich in your bedroom,
because a bird in the sky may carry your words,
and a bird on the wing may report what you say.
(10:16–20)

These verses are mostly about the benefits of wise and honest government by people who take their responsibilities seriously (vv. 16–17). If you are fortunate enough to live in a society with such a healthy culture, you can work hard and avoid the perils of laziness (v. 18).

But then, after two lines of uncontroversial jollity in verse 19, comes the last line: "money is the answer for everything." Unless this is just an innocent comment (that it's always good to have a bit of cash handy), it is surely astonishingly cynical! And it fits with Qoheleth's observations earlier that you'll find corruption everywhere. People with enough money can get whatever they want. Everyone has their price. That's certainly a fact of life in politics and in much of the rest of life.

So what's the point in praising good, sober government (v. 17) and doing honest hard work (v. 18), if, in the end, it's the rich who get all the benefits anyway (v. 19c)? It's still a very relevant question that many of us ask in frustration, anger, and disgust.

So, in a world like that, you'd better watch what you say about the rich and powerful. In fact, be careful what you even think about them—they'll hear, and you'll suffer (v. 20). The egregious wealth of oligarchs and the politicians they "own" is not just toxic to democratic processes, but those leaders can literally poison those who expose and oppose them. And the destructive power of some media moguls is truly frightening to ordinary people who incur their wrath.

Sometimes Investments Pay Off, But Who Knows? (11:1–6)

> *¹Ship your grain across the sea;*
> *after many days you may receive a return.*
> *²Invest in seven ventures, yes, in eight;*
> *you do not know what disaster may come upon*
> *the land.*
>
> *³If clouds are full of water,*
> *they pour rain on the earth.*
> *Whether a tree falls to the south or to the north,*
> *in the place where it falls, there it will lie.*
> *⁴Whoever watches the wind will not plant;*
> *whoever looks at the clouds will not reap.*
>
> *⁵As you do not know the path of the wind,*
> *or how the body is formed in a mother's womb,*
> *so you cannot understand the work of God,*
> *the Maker of all things.*

> [6]*Sow your seed in the morning,*
> *and at evening let your hands not be idle,*
> *for you do not know which will succeed,*
> *whether this or that,*
> *or whether both will do equally well. (11:1–6)*

These are familiar verses, much loved by entrepreneurs. Indeed, my friend Pieter Kwant, for many years the program director for Langham Literature and a publisher himself, says they are among his favorite words of Scripture. Verse 1 is most probably a maritime trading metaphor, as the NIV translates it, since the original "Cast your bread upon the waters" sounds like feeding ducks on a pond. The point is: make your investments, take the risks involved, diversify if you can (v. 2a), and in the end you ought to get a good return. So far so good.

But then the rest of the section paints a series of pictures of the randomness and unpredictability of life in general. Some things you can be sure of (like clouds and rain, v. 3a). But other things you just can't know for sure, like when disaster may strike (v. 2b), any more than you can know whether, when, and where a tree will fall or how and where the wind will blow, etc. (vv. 3b–4).

That leads Qoheleth in verse 5 to affirm an important theological stepping stone toward his final section. He has already proved beyond doubt all through the book that there are limits to our human knowledge, and here he illustrates it yet again from our ignorance of the path of the wind or how a human baby grows in a mother's womb (v. 5a; let's remember he was writing before advances in meteorological science and obstetric medicine). Both of these are wonderful creational facts: the wind does blow and babies do get born, no matter how much or how little we understand of either process. But now he wants to affirm that these very things that *we* cannot understand (including randomness and unpredictability) are all in the hands of *God*. They are all part of "the work of God," the God who is "the Maker of all things" (v. 5b).

Now this is a great and positive thing to say. The whole world, life, the universe, and everything originate in God. So even if God's ultimate purposes are hidden from *our* understanding, we can trust that God is somehow there, present, involved. And with the security of that confidence, we can throw ourselves into life and work as Qoheleth advocates. And yet, of course, while this encourages active faith, it does not remove the problems he has wrestled with all through the book. There is still so much of "the work of God" that remains puzzling, incomprehensible—*hebel*, in a word.

Nevertheless, the strong foundational perspective of verse 5 (the conviction that even what *we* cannot understand can still be the work of *God*) means we can turn life's unpredictabilities not into paralysis, but into opportunities (v. 6). So live adventurously. Don't be idle. Be active, bold, and busy. Make your investments ("sow your seed"). You don't know if this will succeed, or that, or both, or neither, but go for it anyway.

Clearly, Qoheleth has moved on somewhat from the nihilistic fatalism of earlier reflections about the uncertainty of the future to a more robust opportunism. Whereas in his earlier mood he thinks, "We don't know what will happen, so there's no point doing *anything*." Now he's encouraging us with, "We don't know what will happen, so get on and do *something*."

And as we've said before, there is a right kind of Christian opportunism and pragmatism too (Luke 12:35–48; 1 Cor 3:5–15; Eph 5:16; 2 Tim 4:2).

One final point here is to notice the strong creation language of verse 5. God is "the Maker of all things." This is an echo of 7:29 that God made all things (including us ourselves) "right." So the problem lies with us, not with God. The only place to turn, ultimately, is to God—which is what Qoheleth does next, and finally.

"TWO WAYS TO LIVE": REJOICE AND REMEMBER. YES, INDEED! (11:7–12:7)

We come at last to Qoheleth's last words, as reported by the Frame-Narrator. And it is a worthy climax, in which he seems to be making one last great effort to build a bridge between the twin polarities of his quest—his "life-affirming" moments (this will be his seventh) and the "meaningless," *hebel* ones. And he builds that bridge around two words: *Rejoice!* and *Remember!* These dynamic imperatives give us a more potent, and God-centered, "way to live" than the merely conceptual dichotomy between wisdom and folly that he has explored so far.

Let's look first at what seems a reasonable way to understand the structure of what follows (not that Qoheleth is a great one for structure, but we can at least discern some key words that govern substantial portions of content).

> *7Light is sweet,*
> *and it pleases the eyes to see the sun.*
> *8However many years anyone may live,*
> *let them enjoy them all.*
> *But let them remember the days of darkness,*
> *for there will be many.*
> *Everything to come is meaningless.*

He begins with a strong life-affirmation (v. 7), a sentiment with which we can all agree.

Then come two key instructions: *Enjoy* (v. 8a) and *Remember* (v. 8b). These two words then dominate the remaining sections.

- "Enjoy/Rejoice" governs 11:9–10
- "Remember" governs 12:1–7

This provides a framework for somehow holding together both the truth of what he has observed and the truth of what his faith affirms. Life is there to be enjoyed, but as we do so, there are important things to remember.

Enjoy Life Responsibly (11:9–10)

> *⁹You who are young, be happy while you are young,*
> > *and let your heart give you joy in the days of your youth.*
> *Follow the ways of your heart*
> > *and whatever your eyes see,*
> *but know that for all these things*
> > *God will bring you into judgment.*
> *¹⁰So then, banish anxiety from your heart*
> > *and cast off the troubles of your body,*
> > *for youth and vigor are meaningless. (11:7–10)*

Here we have Qoheleth's seventh and final life-affirmation text, and it is strongly positive even if tinged with a dark prospect (v. 8b). Life is to be lived with joy and by following what our heart desires (v. 9a). This is not an excuse for license but a recognition of individual giftings, talents, vocations, and preferences. Follow your heart. Go for what you love!

Don't give in to pessimism and anxiety (v. 10). It sounds like he's preaching to himself, since he has done a lot of that on this journey! In the end, youth and strength are enigmatic in themselves, in the sense that they are transient and sometimes regretted in later life. But while you *are* young, enjoy all the blessings youth brings and the opportunities it gives. Youth is a "time," to add another item to his list of "times" in his poem in 3:1–8, and in the sense suggested there. It is a time is "for" something, something valuable even if it is not permanent, nor an end in itself. Youth is to be valued but not idolized in a hollow "cult of eternal youth." When we do that, we turn it into "vanity."

So then, most of these verses are resonant of the advice given to young people in the traditional wisdom way, as we see repeatedly in Proverbs 1–9. But then, so characteristically, Qoheleth injects a sobering consideration. In all of this enjoyment of life, know that you are accountable to God (v. 9b). God's judgment lies ahead. Be prepared.

This is a key point, and it is crucial that Qoheleth states this conviction before he ends his discourse. For here he affirms what earlier texts have called into question. Remember his bleak musings in 9:1–3? Does it really matter how we live? Does it make any difference in the end whether you lived wisely, religiously, or morally? Will there ultimately be any distinction between the righteous and the wicked? Will there be justice in the end? Back then, Qoheleth left such questions just hanging in the air with a shrug and a "nobody knows."

But now he asserts his faith conviction: *Yes, God will be the final judge, and all our life, work, and enjoyments must be lived in the light of that truth.*

However, we should not take this in a negative way. Qoheleth is not back to his old cynicism here. This is not a kind of "spoilsport" twist. He is not sneering at the young person, "Go on, have your fun now, kid, but you'll pay for it later. . . ." No, he is simply calling for a life lived to the full, with maximum enjoyment of every moment of the present, but a life lived with an eye on the reality of God's presence here and now and into the ultimate future—even beyond death. God is the final auditor and judge. Live life under God. That is not to spoil our lives but to stabilize, enrich, and ennoble them.

And once again, we can say that this note of hearty joy in life and work, lived with full awareness of God, is consistent also with New Testament teaching (Phil 4:4–8; Col 3:17 [probably echoing Eccl 9:10], 23; 1 Thess 5:16–19).

Remember the Story You Are In: The Beginning and the End (12:1–7)

> [1] *Remember your Creator*
>   *in the days of your youth,*
>   *before the days of trouble come*

and the years approach when you will say,
"I find no pleasure in them"—
[2]*before the sun and the light*
and the moon and the stars grow dark,
and the clouds return after the rain;
[3]*when the keepers of the house tremble,*
and the strong men stoop,
when the grinders cease because they are few,
and those looking through the windows grow dim;
[4]*when the doors to the street are closed*
and the sound of grinding fades;
when people rise up at the sound of birds,
but all their songs grow faint;
[5]*when people are afraid of heights*
and of dangers in the streets;
when the almond tree blossoms
and the grasshopper drags itself along
and desire no longer is stirred.
Then people go to their eternal home
and mourners go about the streets.

[6]*Remember him*—*before the silver cord is severed,*
and the golden bowl is broken;
before the pitcher is shattered at the spring,
and the wheel broken at the well,
[7]*and the dust returns to the ground it came from,*
and the spirit returns to God who gave it. (12:1–7)

"Remember your Creator in the days of your youth" (v. 1a) does not excuse those of a later stage in life from obeying the instruction! Qoheleth himself seems to have had moments of forgetting his Creator in the days of his old age, though. Nevertheless, the point is that it is better to be shaped by such "remembering" when it has the power to guide and shape our lives early on.

But what does it mean to "remember" our Creator?

For Old Testament Israel, remembering was far more than just mental recollection. It was an act of covenantal allegiance that called for obedience. It is a very strong word and command in Deuteronomy (read Deut 8, for example), and the Frame-Narrator will apply that point more explicitly in verse 13.

Remembering, for Israel, in the light of the Torah especially (the first five books of the Bible), included at least the following great scriptural truths:

- **Creation** (the scale of God's work is beyond our comprehension, but it is there and it is good, as Qoheleth knew: 3:11; 8:17)
- **Fall** (our own perversity has spoiled what God made upright: 7:29)
- **Abraham** (God's election and promise, the origin of Israel and hope for the nations)
- **Exodus** (God's redeeming love and power)
- **Sinai** (covenant, law, and God's presence in their midst in the tabernacle)

It is noticeable that Qoheleth, like authors in the rest of the wisdom literature, does not mention the last three of those great moments in Israel's story. But he could not have been ignorant of them. He presented himself in the guise of a son of David, a king over Israel in Jerusalem (1:1, 12). So the God he says we must remember as our Creator can only be Yahweh, the God he knew as the Mighty One of Israel, the God of Abraham, Moses, David, and the prophets. He must have known the story he was in. But for some reason not clear to us, he chose to sideline it in his quest to understand the meaning of life through his own wisdom, observation, and experimentation. We'll come back to this point in our conclusion.

But still, in 12:1 he points us back to the beginning (God the

Creator), just as in 11:9b he points us forward to the end (God the Judge). He is aware that the whole of life on earth, including his own frustrating life's quest, is lived within the story that is framed *at both ends* by God. We are in the world that began with God's creation. That is the known past. And we are in the world that will end with God's judgment. That is the known ultimate future. And within that framework, we are called to trust God with the as-yet-unknown penultimate future. *The past and the future belong to God.* The best thing to do in the present, therefore, must be to remember God, trust him as our Creator and Judge, and (as the Frame-Narrator will add) obey his word (v. 13).

In other words, it appears that Qoheleth has finally decided that life has to be lived within the *truth and the tension* of Genesis 1–3—even if he chooses not to persevere any further into the great story of his people. He accepts the double reality of the good creation and the terrible dislocation brought about by human sin. So we simply have to live out the Great Affirmation (the goodness of life, work, marriage, food, drink, satisfaction) in the midst of the Great Enigma (the unknowns, the puzzles, the evils, the absurdities of this world).

That is a struggle, of course. But if we get the foundations of faith right from the start by *remembering our Creator,* in the fullest sense of trusting and obeying him, then it's a struggle we can live with, neither denying that the struggle is there nor pretending that we have all the answers. The *hebel* refrain has not gone away, as the Frame-Narrator sadly reminds us in verse 8. While we have to live now in a world where there is so much we cannot understand, we *can* understand, by faith, that it is the world God created and will ultimately put right.

So at last we come to Qoheleth's closing poem, as it continues through verses 2–7. It is a haunting series of images, which most commentators read as a metaphorical picture of advancing old age and finally death (v. 7). This turns it into a personal warning: build your life on "remembering" God before it's too late, that is, before you die.

Verse 7 echoes Genesis 2:7, with its double reference to dust and breath, or spirit.

> Then the LORD God formed a man from the dust of the ground and breathed into his nostrils the breath of life, and the man became a living being.

But it also echoes Genesis 3:19, God's word of judgment, in the dust of death:

> By the sweat of your brow
>   you will eat your food
> until you return to the ground,
>   since from it you were taken;
> for dust you are
>   and to dust you will return.

We are indeed creatures of dust, but dust that has been given life by the life-giving spirit of God. While that is true of all living creatures that have the breath of life in them (as Genesis affirms [1:24, 30; 6:17; 7:15–16, 22–23] and as Ps 104:29–30 repeats), Qoheleth here assumes that it is the spirit of the human person that takes their personal identity and story somehow back to God when the dust returns to the earth. This at least corrects his gloomy ambivalence in 3:19–21. For if there were not some reality or "means" by which we will personally face God after death, why mention the prospect of God's judgment, as he does in 11:9 and 3:17?[2]

I think this personal interpretation of 12:1–7 (i.e., as a picture of aging and death) is most likely. However, some suggest that the

---

2. Unless one assumes that when Qoheleth talks of God bringing all things into judgment he means only within the span of a person's earthly lifetime. But that is an a priori assumption. It seems to me that the author of Ecclesiastes trusted the sovereign rule of God beyond the horizon of personal death, without having a worked-out theology of "how" or "where."

poem may be a picture of the coming catastrophe under the hand of God's judgment on all evil. Some of the metaphors reflect the kind of disasters that accompany military invasion or the aftermath of a siege and destruction of a city. Some of them are like the pictures the prophets paint of God's judgment when they speak of the day of the Lord. In that case, the warning to humanity would be: Get right with God before he comes in devastating judgment upon the whole world. This is possible, but as I say, my own preference is for the former, more personal interpretation.

Either way, this closing poem suspends our life between the poles of the beginning (creation) and the end (death and God's final judgment). And in either case, God is simply "there," the author and finisher of the story, the Alpha and Omega. "Remember your Creator," then, means *both* to prepare for one's personal death (even in the midst of an active, joyful, adventurous, and hard-working life) *and* to prepare for cosmic judgment. Qoheleth cannot tell us how to do the latter, even if that is what he is hinting at. Only the New Testament will provide a final answer.

This final section of Qoheleth's quest, then, begins with God (12:1) and ends with returning to God (12:7). And that in itself is a remarkable turning point, or end point, of his quest.

Qoheleth has at last, it seems, given up imagining that he can discern the meaning and point of life by his own unaided wisdom and learning alone. It can't be done, and he has found out the hard way. Indeed, when we think of Deuteronomy's strong emphasis on "remembering" God, Qoheleth's attempt to build his worldview on unaided reason and wisdom alone could be called a kind of "forgetting." He had been forgetting the great truths of the Torah and forgetting indeed the very heartbeat of his own wisdom tradition—the fear of the Lord—which the Frame-Narrator will thrust back into the picture in verse 13.

But for now, at the end of his journey, Qoheleth finally puts himself into the framework of the essential biblical faith, which is a story that had a beginning and will have an end. Life is not just meaninglessly circular, as his opening poem might seem to suggest. Rather, life is located within the narrative biblical worldview in which God is the beginning, center, and end. And therefore the God of the story is to be remembered, trusted, and obeyed—*even though* so much of life remains baffling. We still live in a world riddled with *hebel* (v. 8). But we live in it with the consciousness and company of the God who holds its past and its future in his hands and can therefore be trusted in its confusing present.

THE NARRATOR'S LAST WORD (12:8–14)

> [8] *"Meaningless! Meaningless!" says the Teacher.*
>   *"Everything is meaningless!"*
>
> [9] *Not only was the Teacher wise, but he also imparted knowledge to the people. He pondered and searched out and set in order many proverbs.* [10] *The Teacher searched to find just the right words, and what he wrote was upright and true.*
>   [11] *The words of the wise are like goads, their collected sayings like firmly embedded nails—given by one shepherd.* [12] *Be warned, my son, of anything in addition to them.*
>   *Of making many books there is no end, and much study wearies the body.*
>
> [13] *Now all has been heard;*
>   *here is the conclusion of the matter:*
> *Fear God and keep his commandments,*
>   *for this is the duty of all mankind.*
> [14] *For God will bring every deed into judgment,*
>   *including every hidden thing,*
>   *whether it is good or evil.* (12:8–14)

It is probably better to take verse 8 as the beginning of the Frame-Narrator's concluding epilogue, rather than the NIV's decision to add it to the poem of verses 1–7 and then insert the heading, "The Conclusion of the Matter" before verse 9. It seems clear that verse 8 repeats 1:2 and together they form "bookends" for the Frame-Narrator's report of Qoheleth's sayings. It's his way of saying, "This is where I bring my account of Qoheleth's journey to an end. Now let me share my own final thoughts." Notice that he repeats the words, "says the Teacher," with which he introduced Qoheleth at 1:2 and reminded the reader at 7:27.

Verse 8, then, is the voice of the Frame-Narrator summarizing once more the overall theme of Qoheleth's musings. It is not the Frame-Narrator's own final conclusion to the book as a whole (for the text around it is providing some strong counter-affirmations), but rather a framing of Qoheleth's whole quest. "This is what Qoheleth said, and we've now heard the story of his quest. Now he's signing off."

However, even though it seems that Qoheleth has come to a "better place" in his thinking (as we've suggested in our reading of 11:1–12:7), the baffling enigma of *hebel* is still there! It is so important to recognize and accept this.

Faith in the God of the Bible is not just living in blithe and blanket denial, as if bad things don't happen—along with stupid things, things that drive us crazy, things that fill us with anger or grief. They do! They are all around us in this world. And we may never understand why. There are things about time and eternity, about the universe and the ways of God and humanity, that may always remain outside our full grasp (some of which I tried to wrestle with in *The God I Don't Understand*).

But faith—even the struggling faith of a Qoheleth—decisively and intentionally faces up to all that enigma (*apparent meaninglessness*) and sees it enveloped and safely contained within a *bigger meaning*, namely, the biblical story of God, Creator and Judge. And that is the note on which the Frame-Narrator wants to end the book. It sounds as if the Frame-Narrator wants to say two things: (1) *Qoheleth has told the truth*, but (2) *not the whole truth*. He was right at one level, but more must be said to balance the picture. Let's look at both sides.

Qoheleth Was Right! Life Is Baffling (12:9–12)

The Frame-Narrator wraps things up. He has given a full report of Qoheleth's quest and allowed Qoheleth to speak for himself. Now he gives us in verses 9–10 what seems an attractive and complimentary picture of what Qoheleth was trying to do. He acknowledges the immense intellectual struggle and systematic effort. Qoheleth "pondered . . . searched out . . . set in order. . . ." It sounds almost scientific in its rigor. And then, like a conscientious teacher, "he also imparted knowledge to the people," and did so by working hard to "find just the right words." At one level, then, the Frame-Narrator is agreeing with Qoheleth's observation: life on this earth is indeed full of things that are baffling and apparently meaningless. We live in a world we cannot fully understand. *Hebel* is an undeniable dimension of our human existence.

And what's more, he adds, "what he wrote was upright and true." Now that sounds very positive, and it is, but we remember that God said that Job was righteous and spoke the truth (Job 1:8; 2:3; 42:7–8), even though in the course of his discourses Job came out with some astonishing and challenging outbursts and accusations. And that may be why the Frame-Narrator adds the somewhat ambiguous metaphors of verse 11, which have been taken in various ways.

By "the words of the wise," he obviously includes the words of Qoheleth himself. So in what sense are such words "goads"? I think this is the Frame-Narrator's way of warning us, as I've done in a number of places, that we can't just take everything Qoheleth says at face value. As in the book of Job, we have the record of what people said—both Job and his friends—but not everything they say in the heat of the dialogue is affirmed or endorsed by the book as a whole. They may be right in some ways and wrong in others. Similarly, Qoheleth, like the goad on the end of a stick that jolts an animal into action, has been prodding, poking, pricking his listeners or readers with alarming observations, contradictory perspectives, and ironic questions—creating tensions and gaps that we are challenged to resolve or bridge. At times he seems to provoke us with, "So you say you believe *that*. But have you thought about *this*?" He forces us to throw our faith into the furnace of reality and see if it emerges—humbled but still intact.

But what about the "firmly embedded nails"? That sounds like a more positive metaphor, suggesting something that has dependable strength, a structure you can safely lean on, or perhaps hooks that you can securely hang things on. So the "words" may be like goads (prodding you to think more deeply), while the "collected sayings" taken altogether may be like strong nails (giving you something to depend on).

At any rate, the "one shepherd" almost certainly means God (not Qoheleth). So the Frame-Narrator seems to be saying that we need to pay attention to this book as a whole (these "collected sayings") as having its source in God. Even if it is puzzling and disturbing, and even if (like the book of Job) it includes statements that the book as a whole corrects, it comes to us as Scripture, given to us by God.

The warning of verse 12, then, may simply be his way of telling readers not to wander off in search of all the other philosophies you come across in other books. It will be a never-ending and endlessly wearying search.

But Faith Wins (12:13–14)

And so, to the last two verses of the book. The Frame-Narrator has agreed with Qoheleth that life *is* baffling and enigmatic (v. 8). There is so much that shocks and disturbs us, both in what we observe in the wider world and in what may well impact our own personal experience.

But in the end, we are called back to the foundations of our faith. And that is the same as the foundation of all the Bible's wisdom: the fear of God and obedience to his commands (v. 13). This is not only an echo of Proverbs, it is a condensed statement of the theology of Deuteronomy, universalized to "all mankind."

Indeed, the final line of verse 13 is remarkable in scope and potential significance. The words "the duty of" (NIV) are added to help make some sense of the Hebrew, which is simply, "for this [*meaning "to fear God and keep his commandments"*] is the whole human (*'adam*)." If Qoheleth's long search could be construed as an attempt to find out what it really means to be human, then here is his final, four-word answer. This is what being "man" is all about. It is not just a matter of our "duty" but our very identity. The essence of human life is to be found in that relationship with God that has all the relational, ethical, covenantal, personal, and emotional richness that the rest of Scripture attributes to "the fear of God."

So yes, we have permission to *think*, to question, wrestle, argue, ponder, complain. That is one of the great gifts of the wisdom literature, along with the psalms of lament. God *allows* the challenging question, the agonized protest, the genuine bafflement. God gives even a Qoheleth a place in his inspired word! God has a big enough chest for us to beat on and a big enough shoulder for us to cry on.

However, the wisdom tradition stands alongside the psalmists and the prophets in insisting that when we do raise our voices in that way, we do not at the same time raise our fists in defiance, unbelief, and disobedience. No, we embrace our questions and our unknowns with the arms of faith in the living God. We "fear" and we "keep," for that is our human identity, responsibility, and privilege since our creation.

And finally, in his closing verse, the Frame-Narrator states his agreement and re-affirmation of one of the most important things that Qoheleth managed to cling on to—the certainty of God's judgment (v. 14; cf. 3:17 and 11:9b). Nothing escapes God's notice. What may be "hidden"—whether because of human secret sin or because it is simply inscrutable to us—will not be hidden for God. There is no cosmic carpet under which the dirt of history will be swept with impunity. In the end, the Judge of all the earth will do what is right (Gen 18:25) *and will put all things right too.*

And this great concluding truth is negative only for those who persist without repentance or change in a life in which their "every deed" is "evil." It is a gloriously *positive* truth for all who long for truth, justice, and goodness to prevail and who meanwhile live by verse 13. In that sense, the Hebrew *mishpat* ("judgment") in the last verse of the book can have its positive meaning of an action that brings longed-for rectification—putting things right.

That last verse of Ecclesiastes (12:14) is in fact an essential dimension of the biblical gospel. For it is indeed *good news* that evil will not have the last word in God's universe, that evildoers will not "get away with it" forever. This verse points us to the penultimate act in the great drama of Scripture—the final judgment (Rev 18–20), when all evil will be judged and eliminated. It is the final divine rectification, beyond all human justice, when God himself comes to put all things right—the cosmic climax that all creation rejoices to anticipate (Ps 96:10–13; Rom 8:19–21). After which God will make all things new (Rev 21).

Neither Qoheleth nor his Frame-Narrator could glimpse that future new creation in which there will be no more *hebel*, but it is where the closing verse of the book ultimately points.

QUESTIONS FOR REFLECTION AND DISCUSSION

1. In our evangelism, are we too glib in the assurances and promises we make to people without acknowledging the unpredictable stuff of life, from which believers are not exempt (10:1–11:6)? In what ways?
2. What would it look like for us to live as Christians in the world, as people who can enjoy life responsibly (11:8–9) and who also remember and share the story we are in (12:1–7)?

What picture of God would such a way of living offer to the watching world?

3. The book of Ecclesiastes, and especially its ending, challenges us to *accept and live with* the tension between what we firmly believe (e.g., 12:13–14) and what we see and experience in the world (e.g., 12:8). In what ways is this important?

   o **Pastorally:** How does it help us be more sensitive, and less glib, to others in their real struggles?

   o **Evangelistically:** How does it help us to be "real" and handle the questions people throw at us—which are often exactly the ones Ecclesiastes asks?

   o **Personally:** How has this study affected your own faith in the midst of life's journey?

CONCLUSION

Setting Ecclesiastes in the Light
of the Bible's Big Story

Before we leave Ecclesiastes, we need to do one more thing, something already hinted at in our last chapter. We need to lift up our eyes from the text of Ecclesiastes and see the book in the light of the rest of the Bible. We need to do that for every part of Scripture, of course, but it is especially important in a book as enigmatic as this one.

On the one hand, we can look back within the great compendium of the Old Testament Scriptures and consider some of the truths already revealed there, which Qoheleth should have known and remembered as the Israelite he was. And on the other hand, we can look forward along the great biblical story line that leads to the New Testament and consider the great events that he could not know about but that ultimately transform the whole landscape of his struggles.

WHAT HE SHOULD HAVE REMEMBERED

As an Israelite, Qoheleth would have known the Scriptures. Of course, we cannot be dogmatic about how much of what we now call the Old Testament would have been canonical Scriptures in his day or how much of it he might personally have heard or read. But on the majority scholarly assumption that Ecclesiastes is one of the later wisdom texts, then it is very likely that the books of the Torah, along with some scrolls of the prophets and some of the worship of the Psalms, would have been available to him.

So he should have been able to bolster his faith from the promises of God, such as God gave to Adam and Eve (Gen 3:15), or to Noah (Gen 9:1–15), and above all to Abraham (Gen 12:1–3). These would not have answered all his questions or eliminated all the *hebel* he observed around him, but they would have assured him of God's ultimate intention to overcome the evil that stemmed from Genesis 3 and to bring blessing to creation and the nations. Qoheleth does find reassurance in his conviction about the ultimate righteous judgment of God, but he does not seem to find much by way of redemptive hope there.

And he could have taken his lonely searching into the company of some of the psalmists, who often lament the very same evils and injustices in our world. For after they bring these things very vocally into the presence of God and file their complaints with him, they usually find some restoration of their faith and their praise—at least in anticipation. I would love to sit down with Qoheleth and read through Psalm 16 with him, or Psalm 37 (which probably comes from the same wisdom tradition, though Qoheleth might tell the writer of verse 25 that he needed to get out more), or Psalm 73. Perhaps that's good advice for any depressed reader of Ecclesiastes to do as soon as possible after finishing the book!

So then, as is the case with the rest of the wisdom books of the Old Testament, we need to read this one in the light of the whole of the rest of the canon of the Old Testament. As the Frame-Narrator says, what these teachers of wisdom say is *true*, but they do not by any means tell the *whole* truth—and there is a huge difference. For that whole truth we need the rest of the story and the fuller revelation of other Scriptures.

WHAT HE COULD NOT HAVE KNOWN—BUT WE DO

He Did Not Know about the Incarnation

There is a sense in which, as we read through Ecclesiastes, God seems rather distant. He is there, of course—repeatedly. Qoheleth is no atheist. But while he has created and ordered the world in his sovereignty—including all its baffling *hebel*—he does not seem very actively involved in the world of human affairs. It feels as if Qoheleth is challenging God to come down and take a closer look at the mess we have to live in. And even if much of it is our own fault, still there are things we have no control over that just don't make sense. Why does God not come alongside us and feel our pain and share our struggle?

"Oh, that you would rend the heavens and come down!" exclaimed Isaiah (Isa 64:1).

"Amen!" says Qoheleth.

"Don't worry, I will!" comes the quiet voice from heaven's throne.

Little did Qoheleth know that God intended to do exactly that. God would choose to enter into this crazy, fallen, baffling, and infuriating world, which Qoheleth so ruthlessly and honestly describes. God would subject himself to all the limitations and frustrations of a genuinely human life, from a vulnerable birth and infancy to an ignominious and unjust death. God would see for himself in human flesh all the evil, injustice, suffering, unfairness, struggle, frustration, and agonized questions of ordinary people as he lived and worked among them.

The incarnation is God's way of saying to Qoheleth, "I know exactly what you mean. I've been there too."

He Did Not Know about the Cross and Resurrection

As we noted before, Qoheleth complains that often "the righteous . . . get what the wicked deserve" (8:14). But whereas he sees that as a prime example of meaningless *hebel*, God planned to turn that into the central saving act for humanity at the cross of Christ. God himself would endure the ultimate injustice and would defeat the ultimate enemy, death itself. For Qoheleth, death renders everything in life pointless. But for Paul, the death of Christ and his resurrection from the dead remove *hebel* forever (especially the *hebel* of death) and bring us life in all its eternal abundance.

Paul will agree with Qoheleth that the world has indeed been subjected to "frustration" (Rom 8:20). And intentionally, I think, Paul uses the same word, *mataiotēs*, as the Greek translation of Ecclesiastes used for *hebel*. But the hope of the gospel turns that groaning frustration into eager anticipation.

Here is the magnificent gospel answer to Qoheleth's deepest problem. It is the liberating, redeeming good news for all creation. Wouldn't Qoheleth have loved to read this? Don't we?

> [18]I consider that our present sufferings are not worth comparing with the glory that will be revealed in us. [19]For the creation waits in eager expectation for the children of God to be revealed. [20]For the creation was subjected to frustration, not by its own choice, but by the will of the one who subjected it, in hope [21]that the creation itself will be liberated from its bondage to decay and brought into the freedom and glory of the children of God.
>
> [22]We know that the whole creation has been groaning as in the pains of childbirth right up to the present time. [23]Not only so, but we ourselves, who have the firstfruits of the Spirit, groan inwardly as we wait eagerly for our adoption to sonship, the redemption of our bodies. [24]For in this hope we were saved. But hope that is seen is no hope at all. Who hopes for what they already have? [25]But if we hope for what we do not yet have, we wait for it patiently. (Rom. 8:18–25)

He Did Not Know about the Promised New Creation

Well, actually, he could have had some inkling of it from the psalms and prophets, especially a word so explicit as Isaiah's:

> [17]See, I will create
> new heavens and a new earth.

> The former things will not be remembered,
>   nor will they come to mind.
> [18]But be glad and rejoice forever
>   in what I will create. (Isa 65:17–18)

But Qoheleth did not know the glorious expansion of those words that we have in Revelation 21–22. For we can now look forward to the day when Christ returns, when God deals with all evil utterly, finally, and forever; when God establishes his kingdom; when the redeemed nations and kings of the earth bring their glory and splendor into the city of God; when heaven and earth will be reunited as the temple of the new creation in which God will dwell with his people; when our cleansed, renewed and reconciled earth will be the habitat for our resurrection bodies, risen and reigning with Christ; when there will be no more sin, sorrow, tears, or death, no more curse—no more *hebel!*

If only Qoheleth could have known all that!

So then, we must read Ecclesiastes *in the light of the whole Bible story*. But at the same time, we must read the whole Bible *as a story that includes Ecclesiastes* (as well as other books that are tough and challenging, like Lamentations and Job). God has put these books into the whole canon of Scripture for a purpose, and we must take them seriously within that overarching context.

Bringing Ecclesiastes and all its baffled and problematic reflections into the light of the rest of the Bible does *not* mean that we just go away saying, "Oh well, that's all okay then. Things will all work out fine in the end. Jesus is the answer. Stop worrying!" No, the Bible *includes* Ecclesiastes, and it puts Ecclesiastes into a broader perspective, but it does not neutralize or delete its challenging message.

For the fact is, *we still live in the world that Qoheleth describes but cannot understand*. We have to agree with the Frame-Narrator that his empirical observations are true, even if his horizons are limited and his deductions sometimes questionable. And furthermore, we are surrounded in our culture by people who feel the force of the penetrating questions he asks and the bafflement he feels. Many people have said that they find Ecclesiastes an astonishingly "modern" (and even "postmodern") book. It says what many people still think and say. Much of what baffled or offended Qoheleth in his world does the same to most thinking people today.

We do live in a world where so much of our experience profoundly challenges all our attempts to make sense. Even as we heed Qoheleth's biblically justified advice to get on and enjoy all that life gives us by way of work, food and drink, sex, marriage, and fulfilling relationships, we agonize over the baffling mysteries and miseries of our planet. And many in our culture just swing between Qoheleth's two poles—oscillating between a hedonistic affirmation of life (enjoy it while you can) and a nihilistic sense of resignation to the nothingness and pointlessness of our final demise (was it ever worth being alive in this world at all?).

And if we are honest, even as Christians, we often echo the emotions of Ecclesiastes too. The same things in our world puzzle and anger us *even more,* since we know so much more about the love and justice and compassion of God, the God supremely revealed in Jesus Christ. If God is like *that,* why is the world like *this?* How can we bear it? *How can God bear it?* How long, O Lord, how long?

So then, we do need to take Ecclesiastes seriously. It brings us a word that is part of the word of God. It is a disturbing word. A true word.

But it is not the final word.

For the final word will always and only be the Word that was in the beginning with God and was made flesh in Jesus of Nazareth, through whom God was in Christ reconciling the world to himself, and in whom God will ultimately bring all creation to reconciliation, rectification, and unity.

SCRIPTURE INDEX

SUBJECT INDEX